REASONS TO STAY ALIVE

'Far from the tunnel having light at the end of it, it seems like it is blocked at both ends, and you are inside it. So if I could only have known the future, that there would be one far brighter than anything I'd experienced, then one end of that tunnel would have been blown to pieces, and I could have faced the light . . .' At the age of twenty-four, Matt Haig's world caved in. He could see no way to go on living. This is the true story of how he came through crisis, triumphed over the depression that almost destroyed him, and learned to live again.

MATT HAIG

◆

REASONS
TO STAY
ALIVE

Complete and Unabridged

ULVERSCROFT
Leicester

First published in Great Britain in 2015 by
Canongate Books Ltd
Edinburgh

First Large Print Edition
published 2016
by arrangement with
Canongate Books Ltd
Edinburgh

For permissions credits please see p. 245.

06 | 16

A catalogue record for this book is available
from the British Library.

ISBN 978–1–4448–2830–6

Published by
F. A. Thorpe (Publishing)
Anstey, Leicestershire

Set by Words & Graphics Ltd.
Anstey, Leicestershire
Printed and bound in Great Britain by
T. J. International Ltd., Padstow, Cornwall

This book is printed on acid-free paper

For Andrea

This book is impossible

Thirteen years ago I knew this couldn't happen.

I was going to die, you see. Or go mad.

There was no way I would still be here. Sometimes I doubted I would even make the next ten minutes. And the idea that I would be well enough and confident enough to write about it in this way would have been just far too much to believe.

One of the key symptoms of depression is to see no hope. No future. Far from the tunnel having light at the end of it, it seems like it is blocked at both ends, and you are inside it. So if I could have only known the future, that there would be one far brighter than anything I'd experienced, then one end of that tunnel would have been blown to pieces, and I could have faced the light. So the fact that this book exists is proof that depression lies. Depression makes you think things that are wrong.

But depression itself isn't a lie. It is the most real thing I've ever experienced. Of course, it is invisible.

To other people, it sometimes seems like nothing at all. You are walking around with your head on fire and no one can see the flames. And so — as depression is largely unseen and mysterious — it is easy for stigma to survive. Stigma is particularly cruel for depressives, because stigma affects thoughts and depression is a disease of thoughts.

When you are depressed you feel alone, and that no one is going through quite what you are going through. You are so scared of appearing in any way mad you internalise everything, and you are so scared that people will alienate you further you clam up and don't speak about it, which is a shame, as speaking about it helps. Words — spoken or written — are what connect us to the world, and so speaking about it to people, and writing about this stuff, helps connect us to each other, and to our true selves.

I know, I know, we are humans. We are a clandestine species. Unlike other animals we wear clothes and do our procreating behind closed doors. And we are ashamed when things go wrong with us. But we'll grow out of this, and the way we'll do it is by speaking about it. And maybe even through reading and writing about it.

I believe that. Because it was, in part, through reading and writing that I found a kind of salvation from the dark. Ever since I realised that depression lied about the future

I have wanted to write a book about my experience, to tackle depression and anxiety head-on. So this book seeks to do two things. To lessen that stigma, and — the possibly more quixotic ambition — to try and actually convince people that the bottom of the valley never provides the clearest view. I wrote this because the oldest clichés remain the truest. Time heals. The tunnel *does* have light at the end of it, even if we aren't able to see it. And there's a two-for-one offer on clouds and silver linings. Words, just sometimes, can set you free.

A note, before we get fully under way

Minds are unique. They go wrong in unique ways. My mind went wrong in a slightly different way to how other minds go wrong. Our experience overlaps with other people's, but it is never exactly the same experience. Umbrella labels like 'depression' (and 'anxiety' and 'panic disorder' and 'OCD') are useful, but only if we appreciate that people do not all have the same precise experience of such things.

Depression looks different to everyone. Pain is felt in different ways, to different degrees, and provokes different responses. That said, if books had to replicate our exact experience of the world to be useful, the only books worth reading would be written by ourselves.

There is no right or wrong way to have depression, or to have a panic attack, or to feel suicidal. These things just *are*. Misery, like yoga, is not a competitive sport. But I have found over the years that by reading about other people who have suffered, survived and overcome despair I have felt comforted. It has given me hope. I hope this book can do the same.

1
Falling

'But in the end one needs more courage to live than to kill himself.'

— Albert Camus, *A Happy Death*

>

The day I died

I can remember the day the old me died.

It started with a thought. Something was going wrong. That was the start. Before I realised what it was. And then, a second or so later, there was a strange sensation inside my head. Some biological activity in the rear of my skull, not far above my neck. The cerebellum. A pulsing or intense flickering, as though a butterfly was trapped inside, combined with a tingling sensation. I did not yet know of the strange physical effects depression and anxiety would create. I just thought I was about to die. And then my heart started to go. And then *I* started to go. I sank, fast, falling into a new claustrophobic and suffocating reality. And it would be way over a year before I would feel anything like even half-normal again.

Up until that point I'd had no real understanding or awareness of depression, except that I knew my mum had suffered from it for a little while after I was born, and that my great-grandmother on my father's side had ended up committing suicide. So I suppose there had been a family history, but it hadn't been a history I'd thought about much.

Anyway, I was twenty-four years old. I was living in Spain — in one of the more sedate and beautiful corners of the island of Ibiza. It was September. Within a fortnight, I would have to return to London, and reality. After six years of student life and summer jobs. I had put off being an adult for as long as I could, and it had loomed like a cloud. A cloud that was now breaking and raining down on me.

The weirdest thing about a mind is that you can have the most intense things going on in there but no one else can see them. The world shrugs. Your pupils might dilate. You may sound incoherent. Your skin might shine with sweat. And there was no way anyone seeing me in that villa could have known what I was feeling, no way they could have appreciated the strange hell I was living through, or why death seemed such a phenomenally good idea.

★   ★   ★

I stayed in bed for three days. But I didn't sleep. My girlfriend Andrea came in with water at regular intervals, or fruit, which I could hardly eat.

The window was open to let fresh air in, but the room was still and hot. I can remember being stunned that I was still alive. I know that sounds melodramatic, but depression and panic only give you melodramatic thoughts to play with. Anyway, there was no relief. I wanted to be dead. No. That's not quite right. I didn't want to be dead, I just didn't want to be alive. Death was something that scared me. And death only happens to people who have been living. There were infinitely more people who had never been alive. I wanted to be one of those people. That old classic wish. To never have been born. To have been one of the three hundred million sperm that hadn't made it.

(What a gift it was to be normal! We're all walking on these unseen tightropes when really we could slip at any second and come face to face with all the existential horrors that only lie dormant in our minds.)

There was nothing much in this room. There was a bed with a white patternless duvet, and there were white walls. There might have been a picture on the wall but I don't think so. I certainly can't remember one. There was a book by the bed. I picked it up once and put it back down. I couldn't focus for as much as a second. There was no way I could express fully this experience in words, because it was beyond words. Literally, I couldn't speak about it properly.

Words seemed trivial next to this pain.

I remembered worrying about my younger sister, Phoebe. She was in Australia. I worried that she, my closest genetic match, would feel like this. I wanted to speak to her but knew I couldn't. When we were little, at home in Nottinghamshire, we had developed a bedtime communication system of knocking on the wall between our rooms. I now knocked on the mattress, imagining she could hear me all the way through the world.

Knock. Knock. Knock.

★ ★ ★

I didn't have terms like 'depression' or 'panic disorder' in my head. In my laughable naivety I did not really think that what I was experiencing was something that other people had ever felt. Because it was so alien to me I thought it had to be alien to the species.

'Andrea, I'm scared.'

'It's okay. It's going to be okay. It's going to be okay.'

'What's happening to me?'

'I don't know. But it's going to be okay.'

'I don't understand how this can be happening.'

On the third day, I left the room and I left the villa, and I went outside to kill myself.

Why depression is hard to understand

It is invisible.

It is not 'feeling a bit sad'.

It is the wrong word. The word depression makes me think of a flat tyre, something punctured and unmoving. Maybe depression minus anxiety feels like that, but depression laced with terror is not something flat or still. (The poet Melissa Broder once tweeted: 'what idiot called it 'depression' and not 'there are bats living in my chest and they take up a lot of room, ps. I see a shadow'?') At its worst you find yourself wishing, desperately, for any other affliction, any physical pain, because the mind is infinite, and its torments — when they happen — can be equally infinite.

You can be a depressive and be happy, just as you can be a sober alcoholic.

It doesn't always have an obvious cause.

It can affect people — millionaires, people with good hair, happily married people, people who have just landed a promotion, people who can tap dance and do card tricks and strum a guitar, people who have no noticeable pores, people who exude happiness in their status updates — who seem, from the outside, to have no reason to be miserable.

It is mysterious even to those who suffer from it.

A beautiful view

The sun was beating hard. The air smelt of pine and the sea. The sea was right there, just below the cliff. And the cliff edge was only a few steps away. No more than twenty, I would say. The only plan I had was to take twenty-one steps in that direction.

'I want to die.'

There was a lizard near my feet. A real lizard. I felt a kind of judgement. The thing with lizards is that they don't kill themselves. Lizards are survivors. You take off their tail and another grows back. They aren't mopers. They don't get depressed. They just get on with it, however harsh and inhospitable the landscape. I wanted, more than anything, to be that lizard.

The villa was behind me. The nicest place I had ever lived. In front of me, the most glorious view I had ever seen. A sparkling Mediterranean, looking like a turquoise tablecloth scattered with tiny diamonds, fringed by a dramatic coastline of limestone cliffs and small, near-white forbidden beaches. It fit almost everyone's definition of beautiful. And yet, the most beautiful view in the world could not stop me from wanting to kill myself.

A little over a year before I had read a lot of Michel Foucault for my MA. Much of *Madness and Civilization*. The idea that madness should be allowed to be madness. That a fearful, repressive society brands anyone different as ill. But this *was* illness. This wasn't having a crazy thought. This wasn't being a bit wacky. This wasn't reading Borges or listening to Captain Beefheart or smoking a pipe or hallucinating a giant Mars bar. This was pain. I had been okay and now, suddenly, I wasn't. I wasn't well. So I was ill. It didn't matter if it was society or science's fault. I simply did not — *could not* — feel like this a second longer. I had to end myself.

I was going to do it as well. While my girlfriend was in the villa, oblivious, thinking that I had just needed some air.

I walked, counting my steps, then losing count, my mind all over the place.

'Don't chicken out,' I told myself. Or I think I told myself. 'Don't chicken out.'

I made it to the edge of the cliff. I could stop feeling this way simply by taking another step. It was so preposterously easy — a single step — versus the pain of being alive.

★ ★ ★

Now, listen. If you have ever believed a depressive wants to be happy, you are wrong. They could not care less about the luxury of happiness. They just want to feel an absence of pain. To escape a mind on fire, where thoughts blaze and smoke like old possessions lost to arson. To be *normal*. Or, as normal is impossible, to be *empty*. And the only way I could be empty was to stop living. One minus one is zero.

But actually, it wasn't easy. The weird thing about depression is that, even though you might have more suicidal thoughts, the fear of death remains the same. The only difference is that the pain of life has rapidly increased. So when you hear about someone killing themselves it's important to know that death wasn't any less scary for them. It wasn't a 'choice' in the moral sense. To be moralistic about it is to misunderstand.

I stood there for a while. Summoning the courage to die, and then summoning the courage to live. To be. Not to be. Right there, death was so close. An ounce more terror, and the scales would have tipped. There may be a universe in which I took that step, but it isn't this one.

I had a mother and a father and a sister and a girlfriend. That was four people right there who loved me. I wished like mad, in that moment, that I had no one at all. Not a single soul. Love was trapping me here. And they didn't know what it was like, what my head was like. Maybe if they were in my head for ten minutes they'd be like, 'Oh, okay, yes, actually. You should jump. There is no way you should feel this amount of pain. Run and jump and close your eyes and just do it. I mean, if you were on fire I could put a blanket around you, but the flames are invisible. There is nothing we can do. So jump. Or give me a gun and I'll shoot you. Euthanasia.'

But that was not how it worked. If you are depressed your pain is invisible.

Also, if I'm honest, I was scared. What if I didn't die? What if I was just paralysed, and I was trapped, motionless, in that state, for ever?

I think life always provides reasons to not die, if we listen hard enough. Those reasons can stem from the past — the people who raised us, maybe, or friends or lovers — or from the future — the possibilities we would be switching off.

And so I kept living. I turned back towards the villa and ended up throwing up from the stress of it all.

A conversation across time
— part one

THEN ME: I want to die.

NOW ME: Well, you aren't going to.

THEN ME: That is terrible.

NOW ME: No. It is wonderful. Trust me.

THEN ME: I just can't cope with the pain.

NOW ME: I know. But you are going to have to. And it will be worth it.

THEN ME: Why? Is everything perfect in the future?

NOW ME: No. Of course not. Life is never perfect. And I still get depressed from time to time. But I'm at a better place. The pain is never as bad. I've found out who I am. I'm happy. Right now, I am happy. The storm ends. Believe me.

THEN ME: I can't believe you.

NOW ME: Why?

THEN ME: You are from the future, and I have no future.

NOW ME: I just told you . . .

Pills

I had gone days without proper food. I hadn't noticed the hunger because of all the other crazy stuff that was happening to my body and brain. Andrea told me I needed to eat. She went to the fridge and got out a carton of Don Simon gazpacho (in Spain they sell it like fruit juice).

'Drink this,' she said, unscrewing the cap and handing it over.

I took a sip. The moment I tasted it was the moment I realised how hungry I was so I swallowed some more. I'd probably had half the carton before I had to go outside and throw up again. Admittedly, throwing up from drinking Don Simon gazpacho might not be the surest sign of illness in the world, but Andrea wasn't taking her chances.

'Oh God,' she said. 'We're going now.'

'Where?' I said.

'To the medical centre.'

'They'll make me take pills,' I said. 'I can't take pills.'

'Matt. You *need* pills. You are beyond the point at which not taking pills is an option. We're going, okay?'

I added a question mark in there, but I don't really remember it as a question. I don't know what I answered, but I do know that we went to the medical centre. And that I got pills.

The doctor studied my hands. They were shaking. 'So how long did the panic last?'

'It hasn't really stopped. My heart is beating too fast still. I feel weird.' Weird nowhere near covered it. I don't think I added to it, though. Just speaking was an intense effort.

'It is adrenaline. That is all. How is your breathing. Have you hyperventilated?'

'No. It is just my heart. I mean, my breathing feels . . . weird . . . but everything feels weird.'

He felt my heart. He felt it with his hand. Two fingers pressed into my chest. He stopped smiling.

'Are you on drugs?'

'No!'

'Have you taken any?'

'In my life, yes. But not this week. I'd been drinking a lot, though.'

'*Vale, vale, vale,*' he said. 'You need diazepam. Maximum. The most I am able to give for you.' For a doctor in a country where you could get diazepam freely over the counter, like it was paracetamol or ibuprofen, this was quite a significant thing to say. 'This will fix you. I promise.'

* * *

I lay there, and imagined the tablets were working. For a moment panic simmered down to a level of heavy anxiety. But that feeling of momentary relaxation actually triggered more panic. And this was a flood. I felt everything pull away from me, like when Brody is sitting on the beach in *Jaws* and thinks he sees the shark. I was lying there on a sofa but I felt a literal pulling away. As if something was sliding me towards a further distance from reality.

Killer

Suicide is now — in places including the UK and US — a leading cause of death, accounting for over one in a hundred fatalities. According to figures from the World Health Organization, it kills more people than stomach cancer, cirrhosis of the liver, colon cancer, breast cancer, and Alzheimer's. As people who kill themselves are, more often than not, depressives, depression is one of the deadliest diseases on the planet. It kills more people than most other forms of violence — warfare, terrorism, domestic abuse, assault, gun crime — put together.

Even more staggeringly, depression is a disease so bad that people are killing themselves because of it in a way they do not kill themselves with any other illness. Yet people still don't think depression really is *that bad*. If they did, they wouldn't say the things they say.

Things people say to depressives that they don't say in other life-threatening situations

'Come on, I know you've got tuberculosis, but it could be worse. At least no one's died.'

'Why do you think you got cancer of the stomach?'

'Yes, I know, colon cancer is hard, but you want to try living with someone who has got it. Sheesh. Nightmare.'

'Oh, Alzheimer's you say? Oh, tell me about it, I get that all the time.'

'Ah, meningitis. Come on, mind over matter.'

'Yes, yes, your leg *is* on fire, but talking about it all the time isn't going to help things, is it?'

'Okay. Yes. Yes. Maybe your parachute has failed. But chin up.'

Negative placebo

Medication didn't work for me. I think I was partly to blame.

In *Bad Science* Ben Goldacre points out that 'You are a placebo responder. Your body plays tricks on your mind. You cannot be trusted.' This is true, and it can surely work both ways. During that very worst time, when depression co-existed with full-on 24/7 panic disorder, I was scared of everything. I was, quite literally, scared of my shadow. If I looked at an object — shoes, a cushion, a cloud — for long enough then I would see some malevolence inside it, some negative force that, in an earlier and more superstitious century, I might have interpreted as the Devil. But the thing I was most scared of was drugs or anything (alcohol, lack of sleep, sudden news, even a massage) that would change my state of mind.

Later, during lesser bouts of anxiety, I would often find myself enjoying alcohol too much. That soft warm cushioning of existence that is so comforting you end up forgetting the hangover that will ensue. After important meetings I would find myself in bars alone, drinking through the afternoon and nearly missing the last train home. But in 1999 I was years away from being back to this relatively normal level of dysfunction.

It is a strange irony that it was during the period when I most needed my mind to feel better, that I didn't want to actively interfere with my mind. Not because I didn't want to be well again, but because I didn't really believe feeling well again was possible, or far less possible than feeling worse. And worse was terrifying.

So I think part of the problem was that a reverse placebo effect was going on. I would take the diazepam and instantly panic, and the panic increased the moment I felt the drug have any effect at all. Even if it was a good effect.

Months later a similar thing would happen when I started taking St John's Wort. It would even happen to a degree with ibuprofen. So clearly the diazepam wasn't entirely to blame. And diazepam is far from being the strongest medication out there. Yet the feeling and level of disconnection I felt on diazepam is something others claim to feel on it too, and so I think that the drug itself (for me) was at least part of the problem.

Feeling the rain without an umbrella

Medication is an incredibly attractive concept. Not just for the person with depression, or the person running a pharmaceutical firm, but for society as a whole. It underlines the idea we have hammered into us by the hundred thousand TV ads we have seen that everything can be fixed by consuming things. It fosters a just-shut-up-and-take-the-pill approach, and creates an 'us' and 'them' divide, where everyone can relax and feel 'unreason' — to borrow Michel Foucault's favourite word — is being safely neutered in a society which demands we be normal even as it drives us insane.

But anti-depressants and anti-anxiety medication still fill me with fear. It doesn't help that the names — Fluoxetine, Venlafaxine, Propranolol, Zopiclone — sound like sci-fi villains.

The only drugs I ever took that seemed to make me feel a bit better were sleeping pills. I only had one packet of them because we'd bought them in Spain, where the pharmacists wear reassuring white coats and talk like doctors. Dormidina was the brand name, I think. They didn't help me sleep but they helped me be awake without feeling total terror. Or distanced me from that terror. But I also knew that they would be very easy to become addicted to, and that the fear of not taking them could rapidly overtake the fear of taking them.

★　★　★

The sleeping tablets enabled me to function enough to go home. I can remember our last day in Spain. I was now sitting at the table, saying nothing as Andrea explained to the people we were working for and technically living with (it was their villa, but they were rarely there) — Andy and Dawn — that we were going home.

Andy and Dawn were good people. I liked them. They were a few years older than me and Andrea, but they were always easy to be around. They ran the largest party in Ibiza, Manumission, which had begun as a small night in Manchester's gay village a few years before and morphed into a kind of Studio 54 in the Med. By 1999, it was the epicentre of club culture, a magnet for the likes of Kate Moss, Jade Jagger, Irvine Welsh, Jean Paul Gaultier, the Happy Mondays, Fatboy Slim and thousands of European clubbers. It had once seemed like heaven, but now the idea of all that music and all those party people seemed like a nightmare.

But Andy and Dawn didn't want Andrea to leave.

'Why don't you stay here? Matt would be okay. He looks fine.'

'He's not fine,' Andrea answered them. 'He's ill.'

I was — by Ibiza standards at least — not a drug person. I was an alcohol person. A Bukowski-worshipping eternal student who had spent my time on the island sitting down in the sun selling tickets at an outside box office while reading airport novels (during my day job selling tickets, I had befriended a magician named Carl who gave me John Grisham novels in exchange for Margaret Atwood and Nietzsche) and drinking booze. But still, I wished madly I'd never taken anything in my life stronger than a coffee. I certainly wished I hadn't drunk so many bottles of Viña Sol and glasses of vodka and lemon during the last month, or had eaten a few proper breakfasts, or got a bit more sleep.

'He doesn't look ill.' Dawn still had glitter on her face from wherever she had been the night before. The glitter troubled me.

'I'm sorry,' I said, weakly, wishing for a

more visible illness.

Guilt smashed me like a hammer.

I took another sleeping pill and then my afternoon dose of diazepam and we went to the airport. The party was over.

★ ★ ★

While on diazepam or the sleeping pills, I never felt any closer to being 'fixed'. I stayed exactly as ill as ever. The most pills could do, I supposed, was place a distance there. The sleeping pills forced my brain to slow down a bit, but I knew nothing had really changed. Just as, years later, when I was back to drinking alcohol again, I would often cope with lower-level anxiety by getting drunk, all the time knowing that it would be there waiting for me with a hangover on top.

I am reluctant to come out and be anti all pills because I know for some people some pills work. In some cases they seem to numb the pain enough for the good, real work of getting better to happen. In others, they provide a partial long-term solution. Many people can't do without them. In my case, after my disorientating diazepam panic attacks I had been so scared to take pills that I never actually took anything directly for my depression (as opposed to panic and anxiety).

Personally, for me, I am happy that I largely mended myself without the aid of medication, and feel that having to experience the pain minus any 'anaesthetic' meant I got to know my pain very well, and become alert to the subtle upward or downward shifts in my mind. Though I do wonder whether, if I'd had the courage to battle those pill-fearing panic attacks, it could have lessened the pain. It was such relentless, continuous pain that just to think about it now affects my breathing, and my heart can go. I think of being in the passenger seat of a car, as leaden terror swamped me. I had to rise in my seat, my head touching the roof of the car, my body trying to climb out of itself, skin crawling, mind whirring faster than the dark landscape. It would have been good not to have known that kind of terror, and if a pill could have helped, then I should have taken it. If I'd had something to lessen that mental agony (and really that is the word) then maybe it would have been easier to recover from. But by not taking it, I became very in tune with myself. This helped me know what exactly made me feel better (exercise, sunshine, sleep, intense conversation, etc.) and this alertness, an alertness I know from myself and others can be lost via pills, eventually helped me build myself back up from scratch. If I had been dulled or felt that otherness meds can make you feel, things might have been harder.

Here is Professor Jonathan Rottenberg, an evolutionary psychologist and author of *The Depths*, writing in 2014 words that are strangely comforting:

How will we better contain depression? Expect no magic pill. One lesson learned from treating chronic pain is that it is tough to override responses that are hard-wired into the body and mind. Instead, we must follow the economy of mood where it leads, attending to the sources that bring so many into low mood states — think routines that feature too much work and too little sleep. We need broader mood literacy and an awareness of tools that interrupt low mood states before they morph into longer and more severe ones. These tools include altering how we think, the events around us, our relation-ships, and conditions in our bodies (by exercise, medication, or diet).

Life

Seven months before I first swallowed a diazepam tablet I had been in the office of a recruitment agency in central London.

'So what do you want to do with your life?' the recruitment agent asked. She had a long solemn face, like a sculpture on Easter Island.

'I don't know.'

'Do you see yourself as a sales person?'

'Maybe,' I lied. I was mildly hungover. (We were living next to a pub. Three pints of lager and a Black Russian or two was my nightly routine.) I had very little idea of what I wanted to do with my life but I was pretty sure it didn't involve being a sales person.

'To be honest, your CV presents something of a foggy image. But it's April. Not graduate season. So we should be able to find you something.'

And she was right. After a series of disastrous interviews, I got a job selling advertising space for journalist trade paper the *Press Gazette* in Croydon. I was placed under the supervision of an Australian called Iain, who explained to me the fundamentals of selling.

'Have you heard of Aida?' he asked me.

'The opera?'

'What? No. AIDA. Attention. Interest. Desire. Action. The four stages of a sales call. You get their attention, then their interest, then their desire to do something, before they want to commit to an action.'

'Right.'

Then he told me, from nowhere. 'I've got an enormous penis.'

'What?'

'See? I've got your attention.'

'So, I should talk about my penis.'

'No. It was an example.'

'Got it,' I said, staring out of the window at a bleak grey Croydon sky.

I didn't really get on with Iain. True, he asked me to 'join the boys' at lunch, and have a pint and a game of pool. It was all dirty jokes and football and slagging off their girlfriends. I hated it. I hadn't felt this out of place since I was thirteen. The plan — mine and Andrea's — had been to sort our lives out so we didn't have to go back to Ibiza that summer. But one lunch break I felt this intense bleakness inside me as if a cloud had passed over my soul. I literally couldn't stomach another hour phoning people who didn't want to be phoned. So I left the job. Just walked out. I was a failure. A quitter. I had nothing at all on the horizon. I was sliding down, becoming vulnerable to an illness that was waiting in the wings. But I didn't realise it. Or didn't care. I was just thinking of escape.

Infinity

A human body is bigger than it looks. Advances in science and technology have shown that, really, a physical body is a universe in itself. Each of us is made up of roughly a hundred trillion cells. In each of those cells is roughly that same number again of atoms. That is a lot of separate components. Our brains alone have a hundred billion brain cells, give or take a few billion.

Yet most of the time we do not feel the near-infinite nature of our physical selves. We simplify by thinking about ourselves in terms of our larger pieces. Arms, legs, feet, hands, torso, head. Flesh, bones.

A similar thing happens with our minds. In order to cope with living they simplify themselves. They concentrate on one thing at a time. But depression is a kind of quantum physics of thought and emotion. It reveals what is normally hidden. It unravels you, and everything you have known. It turns out that we are not only made of the universe, of 'star-stuff' to borrow Carl Sagan's phrase, but we are as vast and complicated as it too. The evolutionary psychologists might be right. We humans might have evolved too far. The price for being intelligent enough to be the first species to be fully aware of the cosmos might just be a capacity to feel a whole universe's worth of darkness.

The hope that hadn't happened

My mum and dad were at the airport. They stood there looking tired and happy and worried all at once. We hugged. We drove back.

I was better. I was better. I had left my demons behind in the Mediterranean and now I was fine. I was still on sleeping pills and diazepam but I didn't need them. I just needed home. I just needed Mum and Dad. Yes. I was better. I was still a little bit edgy, but I was better. *I was better*.

'We were so worried,' Mum said, and eighty-seven other variations of that theme.

Mum turned around in the passenger seat and looked at me and smiled and the smile had a slightly crumpled quality, her eyes glazed with tears. I felt it. The weight of Mum. The weight of being a son that had gone wrong. The weight of being loved. The weight of being a disappointment. The weight of being a hope that hadn't happened the way it should have.

But.

I was better. A little bit frayed. But that was understandable. I was better, essentially. I could still be the hope. I might end up living until I am ninety-seven. I could be a lawyer or a brain surgeon or a mountaineer or a theatre director yet. It was early days. Early days. Early days.

It was night outside the window. Newark 24. Newark was where I had grown up and where I was going back to. A market town of 40,000 people. It was a place I had only ever wanted to escape, but now I was going back. But that was fine. I thought of my childhood. I thought of happy and unhappy days at school, and the continual battle for self-esteem. 24. I was twenty-four. The road sign seemed to be a statement from fate. Newark 24. *We knew this would happen.* All that was missing was my name.

I remember we had a meal around the kitchen table and I didn't say much, but just enough to prove I was okay and not crazy or depressed. *I was okay. I was not crazy or depressed.*

I think it was a fish pie. I think they had made it especially. Comfort food. It made me feel good. I was sitting around the table eating fish pie. It was half past ten. I went to the downstairs toilet, and pulled the light on with a string. The downstairs bathroom was a kind of dark pink. I pissed, I flushed, and I began to notice my mind was changing.

There was a kind of clouding, a shifting of psychological light.

I was better. I was better. But it only takes a doubt. A drop of ink falls into a clear glass of water and clouds the whole thing. So the moment after I realised I wasn't perfectly well was the moment I realised I was still very ill indeed.

The cyclone

Doubts are like swallows. They follow each other and swarm together. I stared at myself in the mirror. I stared at my face until it was not my face. I went back to the table and sat down and I did not say how I was feeling to anyone. To say how I was feeling would lead to feeling more of what I was feeling. To act normal would be to feel a bit more normal. I acted normal.

'Oh, look at the time,' Mum said, with dramatic urgency. 'I have to get up for school tomorrow.' (She was a head teacher at an infant school.)

'You go to bed,' I said.

'Yes, you go up, Mary,' Andrea said. 'We can sort out the beds and stuff.'

'There's a bed and there's a mattress on the floor in his room, but you are welcome to have our bed if you like for tonight,' said Dad.

'It's okay,' I said. 'We'll be fine.'

Dad squeezed my shoulder before he went to bed. 'It's good to have you here.'

'Yes. It's good to be here.'

I didn't want to cry. Because a) I didn't want him to see me cry, and b) if I cried I

41

would feel worse. So, I didn't cry. I went to bed.

And the next day I woke up, and it was there. The depression and anxiety, both together. People describe depression as a weight, and it can be. It can be a real physical weight, as well as a metaphorical, emotional one. But I don't think weight is the best way to describe what I felt. As I lay there, on the mattress on the floor — I had insisted Andrea sleep on the bed, not out of straightforward chivalry but because that is what I would have done if I was normal — I felt like I was trapped in a cyclone. Outwardly, to others, I would over the next few months look a bit slower than normal, a bit more lethargic, but the experience going on in my mind was always relentlessly and oppressively *fast*.

My symptoms

These were some of the other things I also felt:

Like my reflection showed another person.

A kind of near-aching tingling sensation in my arms, hands, chest, throat and at the back of my head.

An inability to even contemplate the future. (The future was not going to happen, for me anyway.)

Scared of going mad, of being sectioned, of being put in a padded cell in a strait jacket.

Hypochondria.

Separation anxiety.

Agoraphobia.

A continual sense of heavy dread.

Mental exhaustion.

Physical exhaustion.

Like I was useless.

Chest tightness and occasional pain.

Like I was falling even while I was standing still.

Aching limbs.

The occasional inability to speak.

Lost.

Clammy.

An infinite sadness.

An increased sexual imagination. (Fear of death often seems to counterbalance itself with thoughts of sex.)

A sense of being disconnected, of being a cut-out from another reality.

An urge to be someone else/anyone else.

Loss of appetite (I lost two stone in six months).

An inner trembling (I called it a soul-quiver).

As though I was on the verge of a panic attack.

Like I was breathing too-thin air.

Insomnia.

The need to continuously scan for warning signs that I was a) going to die or b) go mad.

Finding such warning signs. And believing them.

The desire to walk, and quickly.

Strange feelings of déjà vu, and things that felt like memories but hadn't happened. At least not to me.

Seeing darkness around the periphery of my vision.

The wish to switch off the nightmarish images I would sometimes see when I closed my eyes.

The desire to step out of myself for a while. A week, a day, an hour. Hell, just for a second.

At the time these experiences felt so weird I thought I was the only person in the history of the world to have ever had them (this was a pre-Wikipedia age), though of course there are millions going through an equivalent experience at any one time. I'd often involuntarily visualise my mind as a kind of vast and dark machine, like something out of a steampunk graphic novel, full of pipes and pedals and levers and hydraulics, emitting sparks and steam and noise.

Adding anxiety to depression is a bit like adding cocaine to alcohol. It presses fast-forward on the whole experience. If you have depression on its own your mind sinks into a swamp and loses momentum, but with anxiety in the cocktail, the swamp is still a swamp but the swamp now has whirlpools in it. The monsters that are there, in the muddy water, continually move like modified alligators at their highest speed. You are continually on guard. You are on guard to the point of collapse every single moment, while desperately trying to keep afloat, to breathe the air that the people on the bank all around you are breathing as easily as anything.

You don't have a second. You don't have a single waking second outside of the fear. That is not an exaggeration. You crave a moment, a single second of not being terrified, but the moment never comes. The illness that you have isn't the illness of a single body part, something you can think *outside of*. If you have a bad back you can say 'my back is killing me', and there will be a kind of separation between the pain and the self. The pain is something other. It attacks and annoys and even eats away at the self but it is still not the self.

But with depression and anxiety the pain isn't something you think about because it *is* thought. You are not your back but you are your thoughts.

If your back hurts it might hurt more by sitting down. If your mind hurts it hurts by thinking. And you feel there is no real, easy equivalent of standing back up. Though often this feeling itself is a lie.

The Bank of Bad Days

When you are very depressed or anxious — unable to leave the house, or the sofa, or to think of anything but the depression — it can be unbearably hard. Bad days come in degrees. They are not all equally bad. And the really bad ones, though horrible to live through, are useful for later. You store them up. A bank of bad days. The day you had to run out of the supermarket. The day you were so depressed your tongue wouldn't move. The day you made your parents cry. The day you nearly threw yourself off a cliff. So if you are having another bad day you can say, *Well, this feels bad, but there have been worse.* And even when you can think of no worse day — when the one you are living is the very worst there has ever been — you at least know the bank exists and that you have made a deposit.

Things depression says to you

Hey, Sad-Sack!

Yes, you!

What are you doing? Why are you trying to get out of bed?

Why are you trying to apply for a job? Who do you think you are? Mark Zuckerberg?

Stay in bed.

You are going to go mad. Like Van Gogh. You might cut off your ear.

Why are you crying?

Because you need to put the washing on?

Hey. Remember your dog, Murdoch? He's dead. Like your grandparents.

Everyone you have ever met will be dead this time next century.

Yep. Everyone you know is just a collection of slowly deteriorating cells.

Look at the people walking outside. Look at them. There. Outside the window. Why can't you be like them?

There's a cushion. Let's just stay here and look at it and contemplate the infinite sadness of cushions.

PS. I've just seen tomorrow. It's even worse.

Facts

When you are trapped inside something that feels so unreal, you look for anything that can give you a sense of your bearings. I craved knowledge. I craved facts. I searched for them like lifebuoys in the sea. But statistics are tricky things.

Things that occur in the mind can often be hidden. Indeed, when I first became ill I spent a lot of energy on looking normal. People often only know someone is suffering if they tell them, and with depression that doesn't always happen, especially if you are male (more on that later). Also, over time, facts have changed. Indeed, whole concepts and words change. Depression didn't used to be depression. It used to be melancholia, and far fewer people suffered from that than they do from current depression. But did they really? Or are people more open about such things?

But anyway, here are some of the facts we have right now.

Suicide is the leading cause of death among men under the age of thirty-five.

Suicide rates vary widely depending on where you are in the world. For instance, if you live in Greenland you are twenty-seven times more likely to kill yourself than if you live in Greece.

A million people a year kill themselves. Between ten and twenty million people a year try to. Worldwide, men are over three times more likely to kill themselves than women.

DEPRESSION FACTS

One in five people get depression at some point in their lives. (Though obviously more than that will suffer from mental illness.)

Anti-depressants are on the rise almost everywhere. Iceland has the highest consumption, followed by Australia, Canada, Denmark, Sweden, Portugal and the UK.

Twice as many women as men will suffer a serious bout of depression in their lives.

Combined anxiety and depression is most common in the UK, followed by anxiety, post-traumatic stress disorder, 'pure' depression, phobias, eating disorders, OCD, and panic disorder.

Women are more likely to seek and receive treatment for mental health problems than men.

The risk of developing depression is about 40 per cent if a biological parent has been diagnosed with the illness.

Sources: World Health Organization, the Guardian, Mind, Black Dog Institute.

The head against the window

I was in my parents' bedroom. On my own. Andrea was downstairs, I think. Anyway, she wasn't with me. I was standing by the window with my head against the glass. It was one of those times when the depression was there on its own, uncoloured by anxiety. It was October. The saddest of months. My parents' street was a popular route into town, so there were a few people walking along the pavement. Some of these people I knew or recognised from my childhood, which had only officially ended six years before. Though maybe it hadn't ended at all.

When you are at the lowest ebb, you imagine — wrongly — that no one else in the world has felt so bad. I prayed to be those people. Any of them. The eighty-year-olds, the eight-year-olds, the women, the men, even their dogs. I craved to exist in their minds. I could not cope with the relentless self-torment any more than I could cope with my hand on a hot stove when I could see buckets of ice all around me. Just the sheer exhaustion of never being able to find mental comfort. Of every positive thought reaching a cul-de-sac before it starts.

I cried.

I had never been one of those males who were scared of tears. I'd been a Cure fan, for God's sake. I'd been emo before it was a term. Yet weirdly, depression didn't make me cry that often, considering how bad it was. I think it was the surreal nature of what I was feeling. The distance. Tears were a kind of language and I felt all language was far away from me. I was beneath tears. Tears were what you shed in purgatory. By the time you were in hell it was too late. The tears burnt to nothing before they began.

But now, they came. And not normal tears either. Not the kind that start behind the eyes. No. These came from the deep. They seemed to come from my gut, my stomach was trembling so much. The dam had burst. And once they came they couldn't stop, even when my dad walked into the bedroom. He looked at me and he couldn't understand, even though it was all too familiar. My mum had suffered from post-natal depression. He came over to me, and saw my face, and the tears were contagious. His eyes went pink and watery. I couldn't remember the last time I'd seen him cry. He said nothing at first but hugged me, and I felt loved, and I tried to gather as much of that love as I could. I needed all of it.

'I'm sorry,' I think I said.

'Come on,' he said, softly. 'You can do this. Come on. You can pull yourself together, Mattie. You're going to have to.'

My dad wasn't a tough dad. He was a gentle, caring, intelligent dad, but he still didn't have the magical ability to see inside my head.

He was right, of course, and I wouldn't have wanted him to say much else, but he had no idea as to how hard that sounded.

To pull myself together.

No one did. From the outside a person sees your physical form, sees that you are a unified mass of atoms and cells. Yet inside you feel like a Big Bang has happened. You feel lost, disintegrated, spread across the universe amid infinite dark space.

'I'll try, Dad, I'll try.'

They were the words he wanted to hear so I gave him them. And I returned to staring out at those ghosts of my childhood.

Pretty normal childhood

Does mental illness just happen, or is it there all along? According to the World Health Organization nearly half of all mental disorders are present in some form before the age of fourteen.

When I became ill at twenty-four it felt like something terribly new and sudden. I had a pretty normal, ordinary childhood. But I never really felt very normal. (Does anyone?) I usually felt anxious.

A typical memory would be me as a ten-year-old, standing on the stairs and asking the babysitter if I could stay with her until my parents came back. I was crying.

She was kind. She let me sit with her. I liked her a lot. She smelt of vanilla and wore baggy t-shirts. She was called Jenny. Jenny the Babysitter Who Lived Up the Street. A decade or so later she would have transformed into Jenny Saville, the Britart star famed for her large-scale painted depictions of naked women.

'Do you think they'll be home soon?'

'Yes,' said Jenny, patiently. 'Of course they will. They're only a mile away. That's not very far, you know?'

I knew.

But I also knew they could have got mugged or killed or eaten by dogs. They weren't, of course. Very few Newark-on-Trent residents ended their Saturday night being eaten by dogs. They came home. But all my childhood, over and over again, I carried on this way. Always inadvertently teaching myself how to be anxious. In a world where possibility is endless, the possibilities for pain and loss and permanent separation are also endless. So fear breeds imagination, and vice versa, on and on and on, until there is nothing left to do except go mad.

★ ★ ★

Then something else. A bit less ordinary, but still in the ballpark. I was thirteen. Me and a friend went over to some girls in our year on the school field. Sat down. One of the girls — one I fancied more than anything — looked at me and then made a disgusted face to her friends. Then she spoke words that I would remember twenty-six years later when I came to write them down in a book. She said: 'Ugh. I don't want *that* sitting next to me. With his spider legs on his face.' She went on to explain, as the ground kept refusing to swallow me up, what she meant.

56

'The hair growing out of his moles. It looks like spiders.'

At about five that afternoon I went into the bathroom at home and used my dad's razor to shave the hairs off my moles. I looked at my face and hated it. I looked at the two most prominent moles on my face.

I picked up my toothbrush and pressed it into my left cheek, right over my largest mole. I clenched my eyes shut and rubbed hard. I brushed and brushed, until there was blood dripping into the sink, until my face was throbbing with heat and pain from the friction.

My mum came in that day and saw me bleeding.

'Matthew, what on earth has happened to your face?'

I held a tissue over the fresh, bleeding scar and mumbled the truth.

★ ★ ★

That night I couldn't sleep. My left cheek throbbed beneath a giant plaster, but that wasn't the reason. I was thinking of school, of explaining away the plaster. I was thinking of that other universe where I was dead. And where the girl would hear I was dead and the guilt would make her cry. A suicidal thought, I suppose. But a comforting one.

My childhood went by. I remained anxious. I felt like an outsider, with my left-wing, middle-class parents in a right-wing, working-class town. At sixteen, I got arrested for shoplifting (hair gel, Crunchie bar) and spent an afternoon in a police cell, but that was a symptom of teen idiocy and wanting to fit in, not depression.

I skateboarded badly, got eclectic grades, cultivated asymmetric hair, carried my virginity around like a medieval curse. Normal stuff.

I didn't totally fit in. I kind of disintegrated around people, and became what they wanted me to be. But paradoxically, I felt an intensity inside me all the time. I didn't know what it was, but it kept building, like water behind a dam. Later, when I was properly depressed and anxious, I saw the illness as an accumulation of all that thwarted intensity. A kind of breaking through. As though, if you find it hard enough to let your self be free, your self breaks in, flooding your mind in an attempt to drown all those failed half-versions of you.

A visit

Paul, my old shoplifting partner in crime, was in my parents' living room. I hadn't seen him in a few years, since school. To me, it might as well have been millennia. He was looking at me like I was my former self. How could he not see the difference?

'Do you want to go out on Saturday night? Come on, mate. Old times' sake.'

The idea was ridiculous. I couldn't leave the house without feeling an infinite terror. 'I can't.'

'What's the matter?'

'I'm just not feeling well. My head's a bit whacked.'

'That's why you need a good night out. If you're feeling down. Get Andrea to come too. Come on, mate.'

'Paul, you don't understand . . . '

I was trapped in a prison. Years before, after spending a few hours in a police cell for that Crunchie bar, I had developed a fear of being locked in places. I never realised how you could be locked inside your own mind.

Act like a man, I told myself. Though I had never really been good at that.

Boys don't cry

I want to talk about being a man.

A staggeringly higher number of men than women kill themselves. In the UK the ratio is 3:1, in Greece 6:1, in the USA 4:1. This is pretty average. According to the World Health Organization, the only countries in the world where more women than men kill themselves are China and Hong Kong. Everywhere else, many more men than women end their own lives. This is especially strange when you think that, according to every official study, about twice as many women experience depression.

So, clearly, in most places there is something about being a man that makes you more likely to kill yourself. And there is also a paradox. If suicide is a symptom of depression (it is), then why do more women suffer depression than men? Why, in other words, is depression more fatal if you are a man rather than a woman?

The fact that suicide rates vary between eras and countries and genders shows that suicide is not set in stone for anyone.

Consider the UK. In 1981, 2,466 women

in the UK took their own lives. Thirty years later that number had almost halved to 1,391. The corresponding figures for men are 4,129 and then 4,590.

So back in 1981, when the Office of National Statistics records began, men were still more likely to kill themselves than women, but only 1.9 times more likely. Now they are 3.5 times more likely.

Why do so many men still kill themselves? What is going wrong?

The common answer is that men, traditionally, see mental illness as a sign of weakness and are reluctant to seek help.

Boys don't cry. But they do. We do. I do. I weep all the time. (I wept this afternoon, watching *Boyhood*.) And boys — and men — do commit suicide. In *White Noise*, Don DeLillo's anxiety-ridden narrator Jack Gladney is tormented by the concept of masculinity and how he measures up: 'What could be more useless than a man who couldn't fix a dripping faucet — fundamentally useless, dead to history, to the messages in his genes?' And what if, instead of a broken faucet it is a broken mind? Then maybe a man who was worried about his manliness would feel he should be able to fix that on his own too, with nothing but silence amid the 'white noise' of modern life, and maybe a few litres of alcohol.

If you are a man or a woman with mental health problems, you are part of a very large and growing group. Many of the greatest and, well, toughest people of all time have suffered from depression. Politicians, astronauts, poets, painters, philosophers, scientists, mathematicians (a hell of a lot of mathematicians), actors, boxers, peace activists, war leaders, and a billion other people fighting their own battles.

You are no less or more of a man or a woman or a human for having depression than you would be for having cancer or cardiovascular disease or a car accident.

So what should we do? Talk. Listen. Encourage talking. Encourage listening. Keep adding to the conversation. Stay on the lookout for those wanting to join in the conversation. Keep reiterating, again and again, that depression is not something you 'admit to', it is not something you have to blush about, it is a human experience. A boy-girl-man-woman-young-old-black-white-gay-straight-rich-poor experience. It is not *you*. It is simply something that happens *to* you. And something that can often be eased by talking. Words. Comfort. Support. It took me more than a decade to be able to talk openly, properly, to everyone, about my experience. I soon discovered the act of talking is in itself a therapy. Where talk exists, so does hope.

2
Landing

' . . . once the storm is over you won't remember how you made it through, how you managed to survive. You won't even be sure, in fact, whether the storm is really over. But one thing is certain. When you come out of the storm you won't be the same person who walked in. That's what this storm's all about.'

— Haruki Murakami, *Kafka on the Shore*

Cherry blossom

A side-effect of depression is sometimes to become obsessed with the functioning of your brain.

During my breakdown, living back with my parents, I used to imagine reaching into my own skull and taking out the parts of it that were making me feel bad. From having spoken to other people with depression, and having even come across it in other books, this seems to be a common fantasy. But which parts would I have taken out? Would I take out a whole solid chunk, or something small and fluid?

Once, during a dip, I sat on a bench in Park Square in Leeds. It was the sedate part of the city centre. Victorian townhouses now turned into legal offices. I stared at a cherry tree and felt flat. Depression, without anxiety. Just a total, desperate flatness. I could hardly move. Of course, Andrea was with me. I didn't tell her how bad I was feeling. I just sat there, looking at the pink blossom and the branches. Wishing my thoughts could float away from my head as easily as the blossom floated from the tree. I started to cry. In public. Wishing I was a cherry tree.

The more you research the science of depression, the more you realise it is still more characterised by what we don't know than what we do. It is 90 per cent mystery.

Unknown unknowns

As Dr David Adam says in his brilliant account of obsessive compulsive disorder, *The Man Who Couldn't Stop*: 'Only a fool or a liar will tell you how the brain works.'

A brain is not a toaster. It is complex. It may only weigh a little over a kilo, but it is a kilo that contains a whole lifetime of memories.

It is worryingly magical, in that it does so much with us still not understanding how or why. It is — like all else — made out of atoms which themselves came into being in stars millions of years ago. Yet more is known about those faraway stars than the processes of our brain, the one item in the whole universe that can think about, well, the whole universe.

A lot of people still believe that depression is about chemical imbalance.

'Incipient insanity was mainly a matter of chemicals,' wrote Kurt Vonnegut, in *Breakfast of Champions*. 'Dwayne Hoover's body was manufacturing certain chemicals which unbalanced his mind.'

It is an attractive idea. And one that has, over the years, been supported by numerous scientific studies.

A lot of the research into the scientific causes of depression has focused on chemicals such as dopamine and, more often, serotonin. Serotonin is a neurotransmitter. That is a type of chemical that sends signals from one area of the brain to the other.

The theory goes that an imbalance in serotonin levels — caused by low brain cell production of serotonin — equates to depression. So it is no surprise that some of the most common anti-depressants, from Prozac down, are SSRIs — selective serotonin reuptake inhibitors — which raise the serotonin levels in your brain.

However, the serotonin theory of depression looks a bit wobbly.

The problem has been highlighted by the emergence of anti-depressants that have no effect on serotonin, and some that do the exact opposite of an SSRI (namely, selective serotonin reuptake *enhancers*, such as tianapetine) which have been shown to be as effective at treating depression. Add to this the fact that serotonin in an active living human brain is a hard thing to measure and you have a very inconclusive picture indeed.

Back in 2008, Ben Goldacre in the *Guardian* was already questioning the serotonin model. 'Quacks from the $600 billion pharma industry sell the idea that depression is caused by low serotonin levels in the brain, and so you need drugs which raise the serotonin levels in your brain . . . That's the serotonin hypothesis. It was always shaky, and the evidence is now hugely contradictory.'

So, annoyingly, scientists aren't all singing from the same hymn sheet. Some don't even believe there *is* a hymn sheet. Others have burnt the hymn sheet and written their own songs.

For instance, a professor of behavioural science at Stanford University called Robert Malenka believes that research needs to be carried out in other areas. Like on the bit of the brain right in the centre, the tiny 'nucleus accumbens'. As this is already known to be responsible for pleasure and addiction, it makes a kind of sense that if it isn't working properly we'll feel the opposite of pleasure — anhedonia. That is the complete inability to feel pleasure, a chief symptom of depression.

It also would mean that the fantasy about reaching into our skulls and taking out the part of our brains that is causing us bother is highly improbable, as we would have to go through the entire frontal cortex to reach this tiny central piece of us.

Maybe looking at a specific part or chemical in the brain is only ever going to give a partial answer. Maybe we should be looking at how we live, and how our minds weren't made for the lives we lead. Human brains — in terms of cognition and emotion and consciousness — are essentially the same as they were at the time of Shakespeare or Jesus or Cleopatra or the Stone Age. They are not evolving with the pace of change. Neolithic humans never had to face emails or breaking news or pop-up ads or Iggy Azalea videos or a self-service checkout at a strip-lit Tesco Metro on a busy Saturday night. Maybe instead of worrying about upgrading technology and slowly allowing ourselves to be cyborgs we should have a little peek at how we could upgrade our ability to cope with all this change.

One thing can be said for sure: we are nowhere near the end of science — especially a baby science like neuroscience. So most of what we know now will be disproved or reassessed in the future. That is how science works, not through blind faith, but continual doubt.

All we can do, for the moment, is really all we need to do — listen to ourselves. When we are trying to get better, the only truth that matters is what works for us. If something works we don't necessarily care *why*. Diazepam didn't work for me. Sleeping pills and St John's Wort and homeopathy didn't fix me either. I have never tried Prozac, because even the idea intensified my panic, so I don't know about that. But then I have never tried cognitive behavioural therapy either. If pills work for you it doesn't really matter if this is to do with serotonin or another process or anything else — keep taking them. Hell, if licking wallpaper does it for you, do that. I am not anti pill. I am pro anything that works and I know pills do work for a lot of people. There may well come a time in the future where I take pills again. For now, I do what I know keeps me just about level. Exercise definitely helps me, as does yoga and absorbing myself in something or someone I love, so I keep doing these things. I suppose, in the absence of universal certainties, we are our own best laboratory.

The brain is the body — part one

We tend to see the brain and the body as separate things. While in previous epochs the heart was at the centre of our being, or at least on an equal footing with the mind, now we have this strange separation where the mind is operating the rest of us, like a man inside a JCB digger.

The whole idea of 'mental health' as something separate to physical health can be misleading, in some ways. So much of what you feel with anxiety and depression happens elsewhere. The heart palpitations, the aching limbs, the sweaty palms, the tingling sensations that often accompany anxiety, for instance. Or the aching limbs and the total-body fatigue that sometimes becomes part of depression.

Psycho

I suppose the first time I really felt my brain was a little bit alien, a bit *other*, was when I was thirteen. It was a few months after the time I had tried to remove my mole with a toothbrush.

I was in the Peak District, in Derbyshire. School trip. The girls were staying in the hostel. The boys were meant to be staying there too but there had been a double-booking, so eight of us boys stayed in the stables outside, a good distance from the warm hotel.

I hated being away from home. This was another of my big anxieties. I wanted to be back in my own bed looking at my poster of Béatrice Dalle, or reading Stephen King's *Christine*.

I lay on a top bunk looking out of the window at the black boggy landscape under a starless sky. I didn't really have any friends among these boys. They talked only about football, which wasn't my specialist subject, and wanking, which was slightly more a specialist subject but not one I felt comfortable discussing in public. So I pretended to be asleep.

There was no teacher with us, here in the stables, and there was a kind of *Lord of the Flies* feeling I didn't like very much. I was tired. We had walked about ten miles that day, a lot of it through peat bogs. Sleep weighed on me, as thick and dark as the land all around.

I woke, to laughing.

Mad, crazed laughing, as if the funniest thing in the world had just happened.

I had talked in my sleep. Nothing is more hilarious to a thirteen-year-old boy than witnessing an unguarded and embarrassing moment of another thirteen-year-old boy.

I had said something incoherent about cows. And Newark. Newark was my home-town, so that was understandable. The cows thing, well, that was weird. There were no cows in the Peak District. I was told I had said, over and over, 'Kelham is in Newark.' (Kelham was a village just outside Newark, where the town council was. My dad worked as an architect there, in the town planning department.) I tried my best to ride the joke. But I was tired, nervous. A school trip was just school, condensed. I had not enjoyed school since I was eleven, when I had been at a village school with a total pupil population of twenty-eight. The school I was at now, Magdalene High School, was a place where I was not very happy. I had spent a lot of the first year faking stomach aches that were rarely believed.

Then I fell asleep again. And when I woke up I was shaking. I was standing up, and I could feel cold air, and there was a considerable amount of blood dripping from my hand. My hand was red and shining with it. There was a shard of glass sticking out of my palm. The window to the stables was smashed in front of me. I felt frightened.

The other boys were all awake, but not laughing now. A teacher was there too. Or was about to be there. My hand had to be bandaged.

I had got out of bed in my sleep. I had shouted out — rather comically — about cows again. ('The cows are coming! The cows are coming!') Then I had gone for a piss next to someone's bed. And then smashed the window. Shortly after, one of the boys shook my arm and I woke up.

It wasn't the first time I had sleepwalked. Over the previous year I had gone into my sister's bedroom and taken books off her shelves, thinking I was in a library. But my sleepwalking had never gone public. Until now.

I gained a new nickname. *Psycho*. I felt like a freak. But it could have been worse. I had loving parents and a few friends and a sister I could chat to for hours. My life was pretty comfortable and ordinary, but sometimes a sense of loneliness would creep over me. I felt lonely. Not depression. Just a version of that wallowy, teenage, no-one-under-stands-me feeling. Of course, I didn't understand me either.

I worried about things. Nuclear war. Ethiopia. The prospect of going on a ferry. I worried all the time. The only thing that didn't worry me was the thing that probably should have: worry itself. It would be eleven years before I had to address that one.

Jenga days

Eleven years after smashing a window in my sleep, during those 'breakdown months' as I'd later call them, there was a lot of empty time to stare worry in the face.

My parents would get up and leave for work and then me and Andrea would have long days in the house. It's weird to write about this period. I mean, really there is nothing to write about. It was, from the outside, the least eventful phase of my life by quite a way.

From the outside, it was me talking with Andrea, either in my childhood bedroom or downstairs in the kitchen. Occasionally we would venture outside for a short walk in the afternoon. We would go either to the nearest corner shop, only about two or three hundred metres away, or — on more adventurous days — we would go and walk by the river Trent, which was a little further away, on the other side of the town centre, and involved me walking through streets I knew so well from childhood. (How could they stay the same when I felt so different?) Sometimes we bought a newspaper and a tin of soup and some bread, and we would return and read a bit of the paper and make the soup. Later, we might help prepare the evening meal. And that was about it. Talking and sitting and walking. It was hardly Lawrence of Arabia. Life at the lowest possible volume two twenty-four-year-olds could manage.

And yet, those days were the most intense I have lived. Those days contained thousands of tiny battles. They are filled with memories so painful I can only now, with the distance of fourteen and a half years, look at them head-on. I was a nervous wreck. People say 'take it one day at a time'. But, I used to think to myself, that is all right for them to say. Days were mountains. A week was a trek across the Himalayas. You see, people say that time is relative, but it really bloody is.

Einstein said the way to understand relativity was to imagine the difference between love and pain. 'When you are courting a nice girl an hour seems like a second. When you sit on a red-hot cinder a second seems like an hour.' Every moment was red-hot. And the only real thing I wished for, beyond feeling better, was for time to move quicker. I would want 9 a.m. to be 10 a.m. I would want the morning to be the afternoon. I would want the 22nd of September to be the 23rd of September. I would want the light to be dark and the dark to be light. I still had the toy globe I'd had as a boy in my room. I sometimes used to stand there and spin it, wishing I was spinning the world deep into the next millennium.

I was as obsessed with time as some people are about money. It was the only weapon I had. I would build up hours and minutes like pounds and pence. In my head, amid all the raging waters of anxiety, this knowledge buoyed like hope. *It is October 3rd, twenty-two days since it happened.*

The longer that time went on, and I was still a) alive and b) not mistaking anyone for a hat, the more I felt like there was a chance I could get through this. But it didn't always work like that. I stacked the days up like Jenga blocks, imagining I was making progress, and then — crash — along would come a five-hour panic attack or a day of total apocalyptic darkness, and those Jenga days would topple back down again.

Warning signs

Warning signs are very hard with depression. It's especially hard for people with no direct experience of depression to know them when they see them. Partly this is because some people are confused about what depression actually *is*. We use 'depressed' as a synonym for 'sad', which is fine, as we use 'starving' as a synonym for 'hungry', though the difference between depression and sadness is the difference between genuine starvation and feeling a bit peckish.

Depression is an illness. Yet it doesn't come with a rash or a cough. It is hard to see, as it is generally invisible. Even though it is a serious illness it is also surprisingly hard for many sufferers to recognise it at first. Not because it doesn't feel bad — it does — but because that bad feeling seems unrecognisable, or can be confused with other things. For instance, if you feel worthless you might think 'I feel worthless because I *am* worthless'. It might be hard to see it as a symptom of an illness. Or even if it is seen as that, it's possible that low self-worth, combined with fatigue, might mean there is little will or ability to vocalise it.

But in any case, these are some of the most frequently cited signs that someone is depressed.

Fatigue — if someone is tired all the time, for no real reason.

Low self-esteem — a hard one for others to spot, especially in those people who aren't that comfortable talking about their feelings. And low self-esteem isn't exactly conducive with getting out there in the world.

'Psychomotor retardation' — in certain cases of depression, slow movements and slow speech may happen.

Loss of appetite (though massive increase in appetite can sometimes be a symptom too).

Irritability (though, to be fair, that can be a sign of *anything*).

Frequent crying episodes.

Anhedonia — I first knew of this word as Woody Allen's original title for the film *Annie Hall*. It means, as I've said, the inability to experience pleasure in anything. Even the pleasurable things, like sunsets and nice food, and watching dubious Chevy Chase comedies from the eighties. That sort of stuff.

Sudden introversion — if someone seems quieter, or more introverted than normal, it could mean they are depressed. (I can remember there were times when I couldn't speak. It felt like I couldn't move my tongue, and talking seemed so utterly pointless. Just as the things other people talked about seemed to belong to another world.)

Demons

The demon sat next to me in the back of the car.

He was real and false all at once. Not a hallucination exactly, and not transparent like a theme park ghost, but there and not there. There when I closed my eyes. There even when I opened them again, a kind of flickering mind-print transferred over reality, but something *imagined* rather than *seen*.

He was short. About three foot. Impish and grey, like a gargoyle on a cathedral, and he was looking up at me, smiling. And then he got up on the seat and started licking my face. He had a long, dry tongue. And he kept on. Lick, lick, lick. He didn't really scare me. I mean, fear was there, obviously. I was living continually inside fear. But the demon didn't send me deeper into terror. If anything, he was a comfort. The licks were caring licks, as if I was one big wound and he was trying to make me better.

The car was heading to the Nottingham Theatre Royal. We were off to see *Swan Lake*. It was the production where all the swans were male. My mother was talking. Andrea was in the front passenger seat, listening with polite patience to my mother. I can't remember what she was saying but I can remember she was talking, because I kept on thinking *This is weird. Mum is talking about Matthew Bourne and her friends who have seen this production and there is a happy demon on the back seat licking my face.*

The licking got a bit more annoying. I tried to switch the demon off, or the idea of the demon, but of course that made it worse. Lick, lick, lick, lick. I couldn't really feel the tongue on my skin, but the idea of the demon licking my face was real enough for my brain to tingle, as if I was being tickled.

The demon laughed. We went into the theatre. Swans danced. I felt my heart speed up. The dark, the confinement, my mother holding my hand, it was all too much. This was it. Everything was over. Except, of course, it wasn't. I stayed in my seat.

Anxiety and depression, that most common mental health cocktail, fuse together in weird ways. I would often close my eyes and see strange things, but now I feel like sometimes those things were only there because one of the things I was scared of was going mad. And if you are mad, then seeing things that aren't there is probably a symptom.

If you are scared when there is nothing to

be scared of, eventually your brain has to give you things. And so that classic expression — 'the only thing to fear is fear itself' — becomes a kind of meaningless taunt. Because fear is enough. It is a monster, in fact.

And, of course —

'Monsters are real,' Stephen King said. 'And ghosts are real too. They live inside us, and sometimes, they win.'

It was dark. The house was silent so we tried to be too.

'I love you,' she whispered.

'I love you,' I whispered back.

We kissed. I felt demons watching us, gathering around us, as we kissed and held each other. And slowly, in my mind, the demons retreated for a while.

Existence

Life is hard. It may be beautiful and wonderful but it is also hard. The way people seem to cope is by not thinking about it too much. But some people are not going to be able to do that. And besides, it is the human condition. We think therefore we are. We know we are going to grow old, get ill and die. We know that is going to happen to everyone we know, everyone we love. But also, we have to remember, the only reason we have love in the first place is because of this. Humans might well be the only species to feel depression as we do, but that is simply because we are a remarkable species, one that has created remarkable things — civilisation, language, stories, love songs. *Chiaroscuro* means a contrast of light and shade. In Renaissance paintings of Jesus, for instance, dark shadow was used to accentuate the light bathing Christ. It is a hard thing to accept, that death and decay and everything bad leads to everything good, but I for one believe it. As Emily Dickinson, eternally great poet and occasionally anxious agoraphobe, said: 'That it will never come again is what makes life so sweet.'

3
Rising

ROY NEARY: Just close your eyes and hold your breath and everything will turn real pretty.
— Steven Spielberg, *Close Encounters of the Third Kind*

Things you think during your first panic attack

1. I am going to die.

2. I am going to go so mad there will be no coming back.

3. This won't end.

4. Everything is going to get worse.

5. No one's heart is meant to beat this fast.

6. I am thinking far too fast.

7. I am trapped.

8. No one has felt this way before. Ever. In the whole of human history.

9. Why are my arms numb?

10. I will never get over this.

Things you think during your 1,000th panic attack

1. Here it comes.
2. I've been here before.
3. But wow, it's still quite bad.
4. I might die.
5. I'm not going to die.
6. I am trapped.
7. This is the worst ever.
8. No, it's not. Remember Spain.
9. Why are my arms numb?
10. I will get over this.

The art of walking on your own

When I was most severely depressed I had quite a vast collection of related mental illnesses. We humans love to compartmentalise things. We love to divide our education system into separate subjects, just as we love to divide our shared planet into nations, and our books into separate genres. But the reality is that things are blurred. Just as being good at mathematics often means someone is good at physics, so having depression means it probably comes with other things. Anxieties, maybe some phobias, a pinch of OCD. (Compulsive swallowing was a big thing with me.)

I also had agoraphobia and separation anxiety for a while.

A measure of progress I had was how far I could walk on my own.

If I was outside, and I wasn't with Andrea or one of my parents, I wasn't able to cope. But rather than avoid these situations, I forced myself into them.

I think this helped. It is quite gruelling, always facing fear and heading into it, but it seemed to work.

On the days when I was feeling very brave, I would say something — ahem — impossibly heroic like 'I am going to go to the shop to get some milk. And Marmite.'

And Andrea would look at me, and say, 'On your *own?*'

'Yes. On my own. I'll be fine.'

It was 1999. Lots of people didn't have mobile phones. So on your own still meant on your own. And so I would hurriedly put on my coat and grab some money and leave the house as quickly as I could, trying to outpace the panic.

And by the time I reached the end of Wellington Road, my parents' street, it would be there, the darkness, whispering at me, and I would turn the corner onto Sleaford Road. Orange-bricked terraces with net curtains. And I would feel a deep level of insecurity, like I was in a shuttle that was leaving the Earth's orbit. It wasn't simply a walk to the shop. It was *Apollo 13*.

'It's okay,' I whispered to myself.

And I would pass a fellow human walking a dog and they would ignore me, or they would frown or — worse — smile, and so I would smile back, and then my head would quickly punish me.

That's the odd thing about depression and anxiety. It acts like an intense fear of happiness, even as you yourself consciously want that happiness more than anything. So if it catches you smiling, even fake smiling, then — well, that stuff's just not allowed and you know it, so here comes ten tons of counterbalance.

The weirdness. That feeling of being outside alone, it was as unnatural as being a roof without walls. I would see the shop up ahead. The letters 'Londis' still looking small and far away. So much sadness and fear to walk through.

There is no way I can do this.

There is no way I can walk to the shop. On my own. And find milk. And Marmite.

If you go back home you will be weaker still. What are you going to do? Go back and be lost and go mad? If you go back the chances of living for ever in a padded cell with white walls is higher than it is already. Do it. Just walk to the shop. It's a shop. You've been walking to the corner shop on your own since you were ten. One foot in front of the other, shoulders back. Breathe.

Then my heart kicked in.

Ignore it.
But listen — boomboomboomboomboom.

Ignore it.
But listen, but listen, but fucking listen.

And the other things.

The mind images, straight out of unmade horror films. The pins-and-needles sensation at the back of my head, then all through my brain. The numb hands and arms. The sense of being physically empty, of dissolving, of being a ghost whose existence was sourced by electric anxiety. And it became hard to breathe. The air thinned. It took massive concentration just to keep control of my breathing.

Just go to the shop, just carry on, just get there.

I got to the shop.

Shops, by the way, were the places I would panic in most, with or without Andrea. Shops caused me intense anxiety. I was never really sure what it was.

Was it the lighting?

Was it the geometric layout of the aisles?

Was it the CCTV cameras?

Was it that the point of brands was to scream for attention, and when you were deeply in tune with your surroundings maybe those screams got to you? A kind of death by Unilever. This was only Londis, hardly a hypermarket. And the door was open, the street was right there, and that street joined on to my parents' street, which contained my parents' house, which contained Andrea, who contained everything. If I was running, I could probably get back there in little over a minute.

I tried to focus. *Coco Pops*. It was hard. *Frosties*. Really hard. *Crunchy Nut Corn-flakes*. *Sugar Puffs*. The honey monster had never looked like an actual monster before. What was I in here for, other than to prove a point to myself?

This is crazy. This is the craziest thing I have ever done.

It's just a shop.

It's just a shop you have been in, on your own, five hundred times before. Get a grip. Get a grip. But on what? There is nothing to grip onto. Everything is slippy. Life is so infinitely hard. It involves a thousand tasks all at once. And I am a thousand different people, all fleeing away from the centre.

The thing I hadn't realised, before I became mentally ill, is the *physical* aspect of it. I mean, even the stuff that happens inside your head is all sensation. My brain tingled, whirred, fluttered and pumped. Much of this action seemed to happen near the rear of my skull, in my occipital lobe, though there was also some fuzzy, TV-static, white-noise feelings going on in my frontal lobe. If you thought too much, maybe you could feel those thoughts happening.

'An infinity of passion can be contained in one minute,' wrote Flaubert, 'like a crowd in a small space.'

Get the fuck out of this shop. It's too much. You can't take this any more. Your brain is going to explode.

Brains don't explode. Life isn't a David Cronenberg movie.

But maybe I could fall the same distance again. Maybe the fall that happened in Ibiza had only landed me halfway. Maybe the actual Underworld was much further down in the basement and I was heading there, and I'd end up like a shell-shocked soldier from a poem, dribbling and howling and lost, unable even to kill myself. And maybe being in this shop was going to send me there.

There was a woman behind the counter. I can still picture her. She was about my age. Maybe she had gone to my school, but I didn't recognise her. She had that kind of dyed red hair that was a bit half-hearted. She was large and pale-skinned and was reading a celebrity magazine. She looked calmer than calm. I wanted to jump ship. I wanted to be her. I wanted to be her so much. Does that sound silly? Of course it does. This whole thing sounds silly.

Indiana Jones and the Temple of Marmite.

I found the Marmite. I grabbed it as an old rap from Eric B. & Rakim played at high speed in my head. 'I'm also a sculpture, born with structure . . . ' I was a sculpture with no structure. A structureless sculpture who still had to get the milk. Rows of milk bottles in a fridge can be as terrifying and unnatural as anything, with the right (wrong) perspective. My parents got semi-skimmed, but the only semi-skimmed here was in pints, not the two-pint ones that they normally got, so I picked up two of the one-pinters, hooking my index finger through the handles and taking them, and the Marmite, to the counter.

Boomboomboomboomboom.

The woman I wanted to be was not particularly fast at her job. I think she was the slowest person there had ever been at her job. I think she may well have been the incentive for the later move towards self-service checkouts in many shops. Even as I wanted to be her, I hated her slowness.

Hurry up, I didn't say. *Do you have any idea of what you are doing?*

I wanted to go back and start my life again at her pace, and then I would not be feeling like this. I needed a slower run-up.

'Do you need a bag?'

I sort of did need a bag, but I couldn't risk slowing her down any more. Standing still was very hard. When every bit of you is panicking, then walking is better than standing.

Something flooded my brain. I closed my eyes. I saw dwarf demons having fun, laughing at me as if my madness was an act at a carnival.

'No. It's okay. I only live around the corner.'

Around the bend.

I paid with a five-pound note. 'Keep the change.'

And she started to realise I was a bit weird and I left the shop and I was out, back into the vast and open world, and I kept walking as fast as I could walk (to break into a run would be a kind of defeat), feeling like a fish on the deck of a boat, needing the water again.

'It's okay, it's okay, it's okay . . . '

I turned the corner and I prayed more than anything not to see someone I knew on Wellington Road. No one. Just emptiness and suburban, semi-detached, late Victorian houses, lined up and staring at each other.

And I got back to number 33, my parents' house, and I rang the bell and Andrea answered and I was inside and there was no relief, because my mind was quick to point out that being relieved about surviving a trip to the corner shop was another confirmation of sickness, not wellness. *But maybe, mind, there would come a day when you could be as slow as the girl in the shop at pointing out such things.*

'You're getting there,' said Andrea.

'Yeah,' I said, and tried so hard to believe it.

'We're going to get you better.'

It's not easy, being there for a depressive.

A conversation across time —
part two

THEN ME: I can't do this.

NOW ME: You think you can't, but you can. You do. You will.

THEN ME: This pain, though. You must have forgotten what it was like. I went on an escalator today, in a shop, and I felt myself disintegrating. It was like the whole universe was pulling me apart. Right there, in John Lewis.

NOW ME: I probably have forgotten, a little bit. But listen, look, I'm here. I'm here now. And I made it. We made it. You just have to hold on.

THEN ME: I so want to believe that you exist. That I don't kill you off.

NOW ME: You didn't. You don't. You won't.

THEN ME: Why would I stay alive? Wouldn't it be better to feel nothing than to feel such pain? Isn't zero worth more than minus one thousand?

NOW ME: Listen, just listen, just get this through your head, okay — you make it, and on the other side of this there is life. L-I-F-E.

You understand? And there will be stuff you enjoy. And just stop worrying about worrying.

Just worry — you can't help that — but don't meta-worry.

THEN ME: You look old. You have crow's feet. Are you starting to lose your hair?

NOW ME: Yes. But remember, we've always worried about this stuff. Can you remember that holiday to the Dordogne when we were ten? We leaned forward into the mirror and started to worry about the lines in our forehead. We were worrying about the visible effects of ageing back then. Because we have always been scared of dying.

THEN ME: Are you still scared of dying?

NOW ME: Yes.

THEN ME: I need a reason to stay alive. I need something strong that will keep me here.

NOW ME: Okay, okay, give me a minute . . .

Reasons to stay alive

1. You are on another planet. No one understands what you are going through. But actually, they do. You don't think they do because the only reference point is yourself. *You* have never felt this way before, and the shock of the descent is traumatising you, but others have been here. You are in a dark, dark land with a population of millions.

2. Things aren't going to get worse. You want to kill yourself. That is as low as it gets. There is only upwards from here.

3. You hate yourself. That is because you are sensitive. Pretty much every human could find a reason to hate themselves if they thought about it as much as you did. We're all total bastards, us humans, but also totally wonderful.

4. So what, you have a label? 'Depressive'. Everyone would have a label if they asked the right professional.

5. That feeling you have, that everything is going to get worse, is just a symptom.

6. Minds have their own weather systems. You are in a hurricane. Hurricanes run out of energy eventually. Hold on.

7. Ignore stigma. Every illness had stigma once. We fear getting ill, and fear tends to lead to prejudice before information. Polio used to be erroneously blamed on poor people, for instance. And depression is often seen as a 'weakness' or personality failing.

8. Nothing lasts for ever. This pain won't last. The pain tells you it will last. Pain lies. Ignore it. Pain is a debt paid off with time.

9. Minds move. Personalities shift. To quote myself, from *The Humans:* 'Your mind is a galaxy. More dark than light. But the light makes it worthwhile. Which is to say, don't kill yourself. Even when the darkness is total. Always know that life is not still. Time is space. You are moving through that galaxy. Wait for the stars.'

10. You will one day experience joy that matches this pain. You will cry euphoric tears at the Beach Boys, you will stare down at a baby's face as she lies asleep in your lap, you will make great friends, you will eat delicious foods you haven't tried

yet, you will be able to look at a view from a high place and not assess the likelihood of dying from falling. There are books you haven't read yet that will enrich you, films you will watch while eating extra-large buckets of popcorn, and you will dance and laugh and have sex and go for runs by the river and have late-night conversations and laugh until it hurts. Life is waiting for you. You might be stuck here for a while, but the world isn't going anywhere. Hang on in there if you can. Life is always worth it.

Love

We are essentially alone. There is no getting around this fact, even if we try and forget it a lot of the time. When we are ill, there is no escape from this truth. Pain, of any kind, is a very isolating experience. My back is playing up right now. I am writing this with my legs up against a wall, and my back lying flat on a sofa. If I sit up normally, hunched over a notepad or a laptop in the classic writer position, my lower back begins to hurt. It doesn't really help me to know, when the pain flares up again, that millions of other people also suffer from back problems.

So why do we bother with love? No matter how much we love someone we are never going to make them, or ourselves, free of pain.

Well, let me tell you something. Something that sounds bland and drippy to the untrained eye, but which — I assure you — is something I believe entirely. Love saved me. Andrea. She saved me. Her love for me and my love for her. Not just once, either. Repeatedly. Over and over.

We had been together five years by the time

I fell ill. What had Andrea gained in that time, since the night before her nineteenth birthday? A continued sense of financial insecurity? An inadequate, alcohol-impaired sex life?

At university our friends always considered us to be a happy couple. And we were, except for the other half of the time when we were an unhappy couple.

The interesting thing was that we were fundamentally different people. Andrea liked lie-ins and early nights, while I was a bad sleeper and a night owl. She had a strong work ethic, and I didn't (not then, though depression strangely has given me one). She liked organisation and I was the most disorganised person she had met. Mixing us together was, in some ways, like mixing chlorine with ammonia. It simply was not a good idea.

But I made her laugh, she said. I was 'fun'. We liked to talk. Both of us, I suppose, were quite shy and private people in our own way. Andrea, particularly, was a social chameleon. This was a kind of kindness. She never could cope if someone felt awkward, and so always bent to meet them as much as she could. I think — if I offered her anything — it was the chance to be herself.

If, as Schopenhauer said, 'we forfeit

three-fourths of ourselves in order to be like other people', then love — at its best — is a way to reclaim those lost parts of ourselves. That freedom we lost somewhere quite early in childhood. Maybe love is just about finding the person you can be your weird self with.

I helped her be her, and she helped me be me. We did this through talking. In our first year together we would very often stay up all night talking. The night would start with us going to the wine shop at the bottom of Sharp Street in Hull (the street my student house was on) and buying a bottle of wine we couldn't afford, and would very often end with us watching breakfast TV on my old Hitachi, which required constant manoeuvring of the aerial to see the picture.

Then a year later we had fun playing grown-ups, buying *The River Café Cookbook* and holding dinner parties at which we would serve up panzanella salads and expensive wines in our damp-infested student flat.

Please do not think this was a perfect relationship. It wasn't. It still isn't. The time we spent living in Ibiza, particularly, now seems to be one long argument.

Just listen to this:

'Matt, wake up.'

'What?'

'Wake up. It's half-nine.'

'So?'

'I've got to be at the office at ten. It's a forty-five-minute drive.'

'So, no one will know. It's Ibiza.'

'You're being selfish.'

'I'm being tired.'

'You're hungover. You were drinking vodka lemon all night.'

'Sorry for having a good time. You should try it.'

'Fuck off. I'm getting in the car.'

'What? You can't leave me in the villa all day. I'll be stranded in the middle of nowhere. There's no food. Just wait ten minutes!'

'I'm going. I'm just so fed up with you.'

'Why?'

'You're the one who wants to be here. My job is what keeps us here. It's why we're in this villa.'

'You work six days a week. Twelve hours a day. They're exploiting you. They're still out clubbing. And no one's in the office till after twelve. They value you because you are a maniac. You bend over backwards for them and treat me like crap.'

'Bye, Matt.'

'Oh fuck off, you're not really going, are you?'

'You selfish cunt.'

'Okay, I'm getting ready . . . *fuck*.'

But the arguments were surface stuff. If you go deep enough under a tidal wave the water is still. That is what we were like. In a way we argued because we knew it would have no fundamental impact. When you can be yourself around someone, you project your dissatisfied self outwards. And in Ibiza, I was that. I was not happy. And part of my personality was this: when I was unhappy, I tried to drown myself in pleasure.

I was — to use the most therapy of terms — in denial. I was denying my unhappiness, even as I was being a tetchy, hungover boyfriend.

There was never a single moment, though, where I would have said — or felt — that I didn't love her. I loved her totally. Friendship-love and love-love. *Philia* and *eros*. I always had done. Though, of the two, that deep and total friendship-love turns out to be the most important. When the depression hit, Andrea was there for me. She'd be kind to me and cross with me in all the right ways.

She was someone I could talk to, someone I could say anything to. Being with her was basically being with an outer version of myself.

The force and fury she'd once only displayed in arguments she now used to steer me better. She accompanied me on trips to doctors. She encouraged me to ring the right helplines. She got us to move into our own place. She encouraged me to read, to write. She earned us money. She gave us time. She handled all the organisational side of my life, the stuff you need to do to tick over.

She filled in the blanks that worry and darkness had left in its wake. She was my mind-double. My life-sitter. My literal other half when half of me had gone. She covered for me, waiting patiently like a war wife, during my absence from myself.

How to be there for someone with depression or anxiety

1. Know that you are needed, and appreciated, even if it seems you are not.

2. Listen.

3. Never say 'pull yourself together' or 'cheer up' unless you're also going to provide detailed, foolproof instructions. (Tough love doesn't work. Turns out that just good old 'love' is enough.)

4. Appreciate that it is an illness. Things will be said that aren't meant.

5. Educate yourself. Understand, above all, that what might seem easy to you — going to a shop, for instance — might be an impossible challenge for a depressive.

6. Don't take anything personally, any more than you would take someone suffering with the flu or chronic fatigue syndrome or arthritis personally. None of this is your fault.

7. Be patient. Understand it isn't going to be easy. Depression ebbs and flows and

moves up and down. It doesn't stay still. Do not take one happy/bad moment as proof of recovery/relapse. Play the long game.

8. Meet them where they are. Ask what you can do. The main thing you can do is just *be there.*

9. Relieve any work/life pressure if that is doable.

10. Where possible, don't make the depressive feel weirder than they already feel. Three days on the sofa? Haven't opened the curtains? Crying over difficult decisions like which pair of socks to wear? So what. No biggie. There is no standard normal. Normal is subjective. There are seven billion versions of normal on this planet.

An inconsequential moment

It came. The moment I was waiting for. Some time in April 2000. It was totally inconsequential. In fact, there is not much to write about. That was the whole point. It was a moment of nothingness, of absent-mindedness, of spending almost ten seconds awake but not actively thinking of my depression or anxiety. I was thinking about work. About trying to get an article published in a newspaper. It wasn't a happy thought, but a neutral one. But it was a break in the clouds, a sign that the sun was still there, somewhere. It was over not much after it began, but when those clouds came back there was hope. There would be a time when those painless seconds would become minutes and hours and maybe even days.

Things that have happened to me that have generated more sympathy than depression

Having tinnitus.

Scalding my hand on an oven, and having to have my hand in a strange ointment-filled glove for a week.

Accidentally setting my leg on fire.

Losing a job.

Breaking a toe.

Being in debt.

Having a river flood our nice new house, causing ten thousand pounds' worth of damage.

Bad Amazon reviews.

Getting the norovirus.

Having to be circumcised when I was eleven.

Lower-back pain.

Having a blackboard fall on me.

Irritable bowel syndrome.

Being a street away from a terrorist attack.

Eczema.

Living in Hull in January.

Relationship break-ups.

Working in a cabbage-packing warehouse.

Working in media sales (okay, that came close).

Consuming a poisoned prawn.

Three-day migraines.

Life on Earth to an alien

It's hard to explain depression to people who haven't suffered from it.

It is like explaining life on Earth to an alien. The reference points just aren't there. You have to resort to metaphors.

You are trapped in a tunnel.

You are at the bottom of the ocean.

You are on fire.

The main thing is the intensity of it. It does not fit within the normal spectrum of emotions. When you are in it, you are really in it. You can't step outside it without stepping outside of life, because it *is* life. It is your life. Every single thing you experience is filtered through it. Consequently, it magnifies everything. At its most extreme, things that an everyday normal person would hardly notice have overwhelming effects. The sun sinks behind a cloud, and you feel that slight change in weather as if a friend has died. You feel the difference between inside and outside as a baby feels the difference between womb and world. You swallow an ibuprofen and your neurotic brain acts like it has taken an overdose of methamphetamine.

Depression, for me, wasn't a dulling but a sharpening, an intensifying, as though I had been living my life in a shell and now the shell wasn't there. It was total exposure. A red-raw, naked mind. A skinned personality. A brain in a jar full of the acid that is experience. What I didn't realise, at the time, what would have seemed incomprehensible to me, was that this state of mind would end up having positive effects as well as negative effects.

I'm not talking about all that What Doesn't Kill You Makes You Stronger stuff. No. That's simply not true. What doesn't kill you very often makes you weaker. What doesn't kill you can leave you limping for the rest of your days. What doesn't kill you can make you scared to leave your house, or even your bedroom, and have you trembling, or mumbling incoherently, or leaning with your head on a window pane, wishing you could return to the time before the thing that didn't kill you.

No.

This isn't a question of strength. Not the stoic, get-on-with-stuff-without-thinking-too-much kind of strength, anyway. It's more of a zooming-in. That sharpening. That switch from the prosaic to the poetic. You know, before the age of twenty-four I hadn't known how bad things could feel, but I hadn't realised how good they could feel either. That shell might be protecting you, but it's also stopping you feeling the full force of that good stuff. Depression might be a hell of a price to pay for waking up to life, and while it is on top of you it is one that could never seem worth paying. Clouds with silver linings are still clouds. But it is quite therapeutic to know that pleasure doesn't just help compensate for pain, it can actually grow out of it.

White space

We spent three long months at my parents' house, then spent the rest of that winter in a cheap flat in a student area of Leeds while Andrea did freelance PR work and I tried not to go mad.

But from, I suppose, April 2000, that good stuff started to become available. The bad stuff was still there. At the start, the bad stuff was there most of the time. The good stuff probably amounted to about 0.0001 per cent of that April. The good stuff was just warm sunshine on my face as Andrea and I walked from our flat in the suburbs to the city centre. It lasted as long as the sunshine was there and then it disappeared. But from that point on I knew it could be accessed. I knew life was available to me again. And so in May 0.0001 per cent became about 0.1 per cent.

I was rising.

Then, at the start of June, we moved to a flat in the city centre.

The thing I liked about it was the light. I liked that the walls were white and that the unnatural laminated floor mimicked the blondest wood and that the square modern windows made up most of the walls and that the low-grade sofa the landlord had put in was turquoise.

Of course, it was still England. It was still Yorkshire. Light was severely rationed. But this was as good as it got on our budget, or just above our budget, and it was certainly better than the student flat with its burgundy carpets and its brown kitchen. Turquoise sofa beat turquoise mould.

Light was everything. Sunshine, windows with the blinds open. Pages with short chapters and lots of white space and

Short.

Paragraphs.

Light was everything.

But so, increasingly, were books. I read and read and read with an intensity I'd never really known before. I mean, I'd always considered myself to be a person who liked books. But there is a difference between liking books and needing them. I *needed* books. They weren't a luxury good during that time in my life. They were a Class A addictive substance. I'd have gladly got into serious debt to read (indeed, I did). I think I read more books in those six months than I had done during five years of university education, and I'd certainly fallen deeper into the worlds conjured on the page.

There is this idea that you either read to escape or you read to find yourself. I don't really see the difference. We find ourselves through the process of escaping. It is not where we are, but where we want to go, and all that. 'Is there no way out of the mind?' Sylvia Path famously asked. I had been interested in this question (what it meant, what the answers might be) ever since I had come across it as a teenager in a book of quotations. If there is a way out, a way that isn't death itself, then the exit route is through words. But rather than leave *the* mind entirely, words help us leave *a* mind, and give us the building blocks to build another one, similar but better, nearby to the old one but with firmer foundations, and very often a better view.

'The object of art is to give life a shape,' said Shakespeare.

And my life — and my mess of a mind — needed shape. I had 'lost the plot'. There was no linear narrative of me. There was just mess and chaos. So yes, I loved external narratives for the hope they offered. Films. TV dramas. And most of all, books. They were, in and of themselves, reasons to stay alive. Every book written is the product of a human mind in a particular state. Add all the books together and you get the end sum of humanity. Every time I read a great book I felt I was reading a kind of map, a treasure map, and the treasure I was being directed to was in actual fact myself. But each map was incomplete, and I would only locate the treasure if I read all the books, and so the process of finding my best self was an endless quest. And books themselves seemed to me to reflect this idea. Which is why the plot of every book ever can be boiled down to 'someone is looking for something'.

One cliché attached to bookish people is that they are lonely, but for me books were my way out of being lonely. If you are the type of person who thinks too much about stuff then there is nothing lonelier in the world than being surrounded by a load of people on a different wavelength.

In my deepest state of depression, I had felt stuck. I felt trapped in quicksand (as a kid that had been my most common nightmare). Books were about movement. They were about quests and journeys. Beginnings and middles and ends, even if not in that order. They were about new chapters. And leaving old ones behind.

And because it was only a few months before that I had lost the point of words, and stories, and even language, I was determined never to feel like that again. I fed and I fed and I fed.

I used to sit with the bedside lamp on, reading for about two hours after Andrea had gone to sleep, until my eyes were dry and sore, always seeking and never quite finding, but with that feeling of being tantalisingly close.

The Power and the Glory

One of the books I remember (re-)reading was *The Power and the Glory* by Graham Greene.

Graham Greene was an interesting choice. I had studied the writer while doing an MA at Leeds University. I don't know why I took that module. I didn't really know anything about Graham Greene. I knew about *Brighton Rock* but I'd never read it. I'd also heard once that he'd lived in Nottinghamshire and hated it. I had lived in Nottinghamshire and — at that time — had often hated it too. Maybe that was the reason.

For the first few weeks I'd thought it was a major mistake. I was the only person who'd taken the module. And the tutor hated me. I don't know if 'hate' is the word, but he certainly didn't *like* me. He was a Catholic, always dressed formally, and spoke to me with delicate disdain.

Those hours were long, and had all the relaxed and casual joy of a trip to the doctor's for a testicular inspection. Often I must have stank of beer, as I would always drink a can or two on the train journey to Leeds (from

Hull, where Andrea and I were still living). At the end of the module I wrote the best essay I had ever written, and was given a 69 per cent. One shy of a distinction. I took it as a personal insult.

Anyway, I loved Graham Greene. His works were filled with a discomfort I related to. There were all kinds of discomforts on offer. Discomforts of guilt, sex, Catholicism, unrequited love, forbidden lust, tropical heat, politics, war. Everything was uncomfortable, except the prose.

I loved the way he wrote. I loved the way he'd compare a solid thing to something abstract. 'He drank the brandy down like damnation.' I loved this technique even more now, because the divide between the material and non-material worlds seemed to have blurred. With depression. Even my own physical body seemed unreal and abstract and partly fictional.

The Power and the Glory is about a 'whisky priest' travelling through Mexico in the 1930s, at a time when Catholicism is outlawed. Throughout the novel he is pursued by a police lieutenant tasked with tracking him down.

I had liked this story when I first read it at university, but I loved it now. Having been a borderline alcoholic in Ibiza, empathising with a borderline alcoholic in Mexico wasn't too hard.

It is a dark, intense book. But when you are feeling dark and intense these are the only kind of books that can speak to you. Yet there was an optimism too. The possibility of redemption. It is a book about the healing power of love.

'Hate is a lack of imagination,' we are told.

But also: 'There is always one moment in childhood when the door opens and lets the future in.' Experience surrounds innocence and innocence can never be regained once lost. The book is about — like many of his books — Catholic guilt. But for me it was about depression. Greene was a depressive. Had been since a child, being bullied at the school where his unpopular father was headmaster. He'd semi-attempted suicide with a solitary game of Russian roulette. The guilt was — for me — not the spiritual guilt of Catholicism but the psychological guilt that depression brings. And it helped relieve the isolation that the illness brings.

★   ★   ★

Other books I read at this time:

Invisible Cities, Italo Calvino — The most beautiful book. Imaginary cities, each kind of like Venice but not at all like Venice. Dreams on a page. So unreal they could almost dislodge my strange mind-visions.

The Outsiders, S.E. Hinton — The book that got me properly into reading as a ten-year-old. Has always been my favourite 'escape' read. It drips with America and has gorgeously sentimental dialogue. (Like: 'Stay gold, Ponyboy', said by Johnny, on his death bed, after reading Robert Frost's 'Nothing Gold Can Stay'.)

The Outsider, Albert Camus — I had a thing about outsiders. And existential despair. The numbness of the prose was strangely soothing.

The Concise Collins Dictionary of Quotations — Quotations are easy to read.

Letters of Keats — I had studied Keats at university. The archetypal young poet was thin-skinned and doomed and intense, and I felt these things.

Oranges Are Not the Only Fruit, Jeanette Winterson — I loved Jeanette's writing. Every word contained strength or wisdom. I picked it up at random pages to see sentences that could speak to me. 'I seem to have run in a great circle, and met myself again on the starting line.'

Vox, Nicholson Baker — A novel that consists entirely of an episode of phone sex, that had titillated and enthralled me when I was sixteen. Pure dialogue. Again, easy to read, and full of sex, or the idea of sex, and for a young, anxiety-riddled mind, thinking of sex can be a positive distraction.

Money, Martin Amis — *Money* was a book I knew inside out. I'd done essays on it. It was full of ballsy, swaggering, sharp, funny, macho (though sometimes rather hateful) prose. There was an intensity to it. And sad beauty amid the comedy. ('Every hour you get weaker. Sometimes, as I sit alone in my flat in London and stare at the window, I think how dismal it is, how heavy, to watch the rain and not know why it falls.')

The Diary of Samuel Pepys — In particular, I'd read the bit about the Great Fire and the plague. There was something about the way Pepys jollied on through the more apocalyptic events of seventeenth-century life that was very therapeutic to read about.

The Catcher in the Rye, J.D. Salinger — Because Holden was an old friend.

The Penguin Book of First World War Poetry — Poems like Ivor Gurney's 'Strange Hells' ('The heart burns — but has to keep out of face how heart burns') and Wilfred Owen's 'Mental Cases' (describing the shell-shocked patients of a mental hospital) fascinated me but troubled me. I had been through no war and yet I related to that feeling of pain contained in every new day, as 'Dawn breaks open like a wound that bleeds afresh'. It fascinated me how depression and anxiety overlap with post-traumatic stress disorder. Had we been through some trauma we didn't know about? Was the noise and speed of modern life the trauma for our caveman brains? Was I that soft? Or was life a kind of war most people didn't see?

A History of the World in Ten and a Half Chapters, Julian Barnes — Just because it was a book I had read and loved before and which was funny and strange and I knew it inside out.

Wilderness Tips, Margaret Atwood — Short stories. Smaller hills to climb. A story called 'True Trash' was my favourite. About teenage boys perving at waitresses.

Wide Sargasso Sea, Jean Rhys — A prequel to *Jane Eyre*. About the 'madwoman in the attic' and her descent into madness. It is mainly set in the Caribbean. The despair and isolation felt in paradise was what I related to most, to feeling terrible 'in the most beautiful place in the world', which reminded me of that last week in Spain.

Paris

She was about to tell me my birthday surprise.

'We're going to Paris. Tomorrow. We're going to Paris tomorrow! We're going to get the Eurostar.'

I was shell-shocked. I couldn't imagine anyone saying anything more terrifying. 'I can't. I can't go to Paris.'

It was happening. A panic attack. I was starting to feel it in my chest. I was starting to feel like I was back in 2000 mode. Back in that feeling of being trapped inside my self, like a desperate fly in a jar.

'Well, we're going. We're staying in the sixth. It's going to be great. We're staying in the hotel Oscar Wilde died in. L'Hotel, it's called.'

Going to the place where Oscar Wilde died wasn't making it any better. It just guaranteed I was going to die there. To die in Paris, just like Oscar Wilde. I also imagined the air would kill me. I hadn't been abroad for four years.

'I don't think I'll be able to breathe the air.' I knew this sounded stupid. I wasn't mad!

And yet, the fact remained: *I didn't think I'd be able to breathe the air.*

At some point after that I was curled tight in a foetal ball behind the door. I was trembling. I don't know if anyone had been this scared of Paris since Marie Antoinette. But Andrea knew what to do. She had a PhD in this kind of thing by now. She said: 'Okay, we won't go. I can cancel the hotel. We might lose a bit of money, but if it's such a big deal . . . '

Such a big deal.

I could still hardly walk twenty metres on my own without having a panic attack. It was the biggest deal imaginable. It was like, I suppose, a normal person being told they had to walk naked around Tehran or something.

But.

If I said 'no', then I would be a person who couldn't travel abroad because he was scared. And that would make me like a mad person, and my biggest fear — bigger even than death — was of being totally mad. Of losing myself completely to the demons. So, as was so often the case, a big fear was beaten by a bigger fear.

The best way to beat a monster is to find a scarier one.

And I went to Paris. The Channel tunnel held together and the sea didn't fall on our heads. The air in Paris worked okay with my lungs. Though I could hardly speak in the taxi. The journey from Gare du Nord to the hotel was intense. There was some kind of march going on by the banks of the Seine, with a large red flag swooping like the Tricolore in *Les Miserables*.

When I closed my eyes that night I couldn't sleep for hours because I kept seeing Paris moving at the speed it had moved by in the taxi. But I calmed. I didn't actually have a proper panic attack at any point during the next four days. Just a generalised high anxiety that I felt walking around the Left Bank and along the Rue de Rivoli and in the restaurant on the roof of the Pompidou Centre. I was starting to find that, sometimes, simply doing something that I had dreaded — and surviving — was the best kind of therapy. If you start to dread being outside, go outside. If you fear confined spaces, spend some time in a lift. If you have separation anxiety, force yourself to be alone a while. When you are depressed and anxious your comfort zone tends to shrink from the size of a world to the size of a bed. Or right down to nothing at all.

Another thing. Stimulation. Excitement. The kinds found in new places. Sometimes this can be terrifying, but it can also be liberating. In a familiar place, your mind focuses solely on itself. There is nothing new it needs to notice about your bedroom. No potential external threats, just internal ones. By forcing yourself into a new physical space, preferably in a different country, you end up inevitably focusing a bit more on the world outside your head.

Well, that's how it worked for me. Those few days in Paris.

In fact, I felt more normal than I did at home, because here my general anxious awkwardness could pass quite easily for general awkward Britishness.

A lot of depressed people turn to travel as an antidote to their symptoms. The great American painter Georgia O'Keeffe, like the many other artists that fit the cliché, was a life-long depressive. In 1933, at the age of forty-six, she was hospitalised following symptoms of uncontrollable crying, a seeming inability to eat or sleep, and other symptoms of depression and anxiety.

O'Keeffe's biographer Roxana Robinson says that the hospital stay did little for her. What worked instead was travel. She went to Bermuda and Lake George in New York and Maine and Hawaii. 'Warmth, languor, and solitude were just what Georgia needed,' wrote Robinson.

Of course, travel isn't always a solution. Or

even an option. But it certainly helps me, when I get the chance to go away. I think, more than anything, it helps give a sense of perspective. We might be stuck in our minds, but we aren't physically stuck. And unsticking ourselves from our physical location can help dislodge our unhappy mental state. Movement is the antidote to fixedness, after all. And it helps. Sometimes. Just sometimes.

'Travel makes one modest,' said Gustave Flaubert. 'You see what a tiny place you occupy in the world.' Such perspective can be strangely liberating. Especially when you have an illness that may on the one hand lower self-esteem, but on the other intensifies the trivial.

I can remember during a short depressive episode watching Martin Scorsese's Howard Hughes biopic *The Aviator*. There is a point in it where Katharine Hepburn, played rather brilliantly by Cate Blanchett, turns to Hughes (Leonardo DiCaprio) and says: 'There's too much Howard Hughes in Howard Hughes.' It was this intensity of the self that, in the film version of his life at least, was shown to contribute to the obsessive-compulsive disorder that would eventually imprison Hughes in a hotel room in Las Vegas.

Andrea told me after that film that there was too much Matt Haig in Matt Haig. She was kind of joking, but also kind of on to something. So for me, anything that lessens that extreme sense of self, that makes me feel me but at a lower volume, is very welcome. And ever since that Paris trip, travel has been one of those things.

Reasons to be strong

It was 2002. I was at that point in my recovery where I was continually feeling well, but only in contrast to the much worse stuff that had gone before. Really, I was still a walking mass of anxiety, too phobic to take medicine of any kind, and convinced my tongue was expanding every time I consumed prawns or peanut butter or any other food it is possible to be allergic to. I also needed to be near Andrea. If I was near Andrea I was infinitely calmer than when I wasn't.

Most of the time, this didn't make me feel like a weirdo. Me and Andrea lived together and worked together in the same modest apartment. We did not really know anyone socially. Out of the two of us, I had always been the one with the drive to go out and meet other people, and that drive had gone now.

But in 2002 Andrea's mother was diagnosed with ovarian cancer and things understandably changed. We went and stayed with her parents in County Durham while Freda underwent chemotherapy. Andrea, who had spent the last three years fixing a depressive boyfriend, now had a mother with cancer.

She cried a lot. I felt like the baton was being passed. This was my turn to be the strong one.

When she first found out her mum was ill she sat on the edge of the bed and cried like I had never seen her cry. I put my arm around her and felt that sudden shrinking of language you feel when something terrible happens. Fortunately, Andrea was on hand to help.

'Just say it's going to be okay,' she said.

'It's going to be okay.'

Two months later, I was alone in the house of my future in-laws, pleading with Andrea to go with them to the hospital.

'I've got to take Mum to hospital,' she had said.

'Okay. I'll come with you.'

'They want someone to wait and let David in.' David was Andrea's brother, travelling up from London.

'I can come with you.'

'Matt, please.'

'I can't do this. Separation anxiety. I'll have a panic attack.'

'Matt, I'm asking you. My mum's ill. I don't want to stress her out. You're being selfish.'

'Fuck. Shit. I'm sorry. But you don't understand.'

'You can do this.'

'I won't make it. Can't you just tell your mum and dad I've got to come too?'

'Okay. All right. Okay. I will.'

But then it happened. A switch flicked. 'No.'

'No what?'

'I'll do it. I'll stay. I'll stay in the house.'

'Really?'

'Yeah.'

'I'll leave the number for the hospital.'

'It's okay,' I said, stupidly imagining these could be my last ever words to her. 'I could find it.'

'I'll leave it anyway.'

'Thank you.'

'It's okay. You'd better go.'

While waiting for them to come home with Andrea from the hospital I paced from room to room. They had lots of porcelain ornaments. Little Bo Peep. A Pink Panther sitting cross-legged, his legs hanging down off the windowsill. His wide yellow eyes followed me around the living room.

The first ten minutes my heart was pounding. I could hardly breathe. Andrea was dead. Her parents were dead. I was picturing the car crash too vividly for it not to have happened. Then twenty minutes passed. I was going to die. There was a pain in my chest. Maybe it was lung cancer. I was only twenty-seven, but I had smoked a lot. At thirty minutes, a neighbour came around to see how Freda was. At forty minutes, the adrenaline was starting to settle. I had been forty minutes on my own and I was still alive. By fifty minutes, I actually wanted them to be gone over an hour, so that I could feel even stronger. Fifty minutes! Three years of separation anxiety cured in less than an hour!

Needless to say, they came back.

* * *

It was a horrible summer, but the outcome was okay. Andrea's mother was given terrible odds, but she beat them. We even managed to replace her daily breakfast of a biscuit with a kiwi fruit. I had reasons to force myself to be strong. To put myself in situations I wouldn't have put myself in. You need to be uncomfortable. You need to hurt. As the Persian poet Rumi wrote in the twelfth century, 'The wound is the place where the light enters you.' (He also wrote: 'Forget safety. Live where you fear to live.') Also, I channelled my mind by writing my first proper novel. Not principally for career reasons (the novel was a reworking of Shakespeare's *Henry IV*, with talking dogs, so hardly bestseller territory), but to occupy myself. Two years later, though, and with Andrea's encouragement, it would be an actual published book. I dedicated the book to Andrea, obviously, but it wasn't just a book I owed her. It was a whole life.

Weapons

My agent. 'You've got a publisher.'

'What?'

'Just had the phone call. You are going to be a published author.'

'*What? Seriously?*'

'Seriously.'

This news kept me going for about six months.

For about six months my lack of self-esteem had been artificially addressed. I would lie in bed and go to sleep smiling, thinking *Wow, I'm quite a big deal, I'm going to be published.*

But being published (or getting a great job or whatever) does not permanently alter your brain. And one night I lay awake, feeling less than happy. I started to worry. The worries spiralled. And for three weeks I was trapped in my own mind again. But this time, I had weapons. One of them, maybe the most important, was this knowledge: *I have been ill before, then well again. Wellness is possible.* Another weapon was running. I knew how the body could affect the mind, so I started to run more and more.

Running

Running is a commonly cited alleviator of depression and anxiety. It certainly worked for me. When I started running I was still getting very bad panic attacks. The thing I liked about it was that many of the physical symptoms of panic — the racing heart, the problematic breathing, the sweating — are matched by running. So while I was running I wouldn't be worried about my racing heart because it had a reason to be racing.

Also, it gave me something to think about. I was never exactly the fittest person in the world, so running was quite difficult. It hurt. But that effort and discomfort was a great focuser. And so I convinced myself that through training my body I was also training my mind. It was a kind of active meditation.

It also, of course, gets you fit. And getting fit is pretty much good for everything. When I became ill I had been drinking and smoking heavily, but now I was trying to undo that damage.

So every day I would go running, or do an equivalent type of cardiovascular exercise. Like Haruki Murakami — whose excellent book *What I Talk About When I Talk About Running* I would later read — I found running to be a way of clearing the fog. ('Exerting yourself to the fullest within your individual limits: that's the essence of running,' Murakami also said, which is something I've come to believe too, and is one of the reasons I believe it helps the mind.)

I would come back from a run and stretch and have a shower and feel a gentle sense of release, as though depression and anxiety were slowly evaporating from inside me. It was a wonderful feeling. Also, that kind of monotony that running generates — the one soundtracked by heavy breathing and the steady rhythm of feet on pavements — became a kind of metaphor for depression. To go on a run every day is to have a kind of battle with yourself. Just getting out on a cold February morning gives you a sense of achievement. But that voiceless debate you have with yourself — *I want to stop! No, keep going! I can't, I can hardly breathe! There's only a mile to go! I just need to lie down! You can't!* — is the debate of depression, but on a smaller and less serious scale. So for me, each time I forced myself out there in the cold grey damp of a West Yorkshire morning, and pushed myself to run for an hour, it gave me a little bit of depression-beating power. A little bit of that 'you'd better be careful with who you are messing with' spirit.

It helped, sometimes. Not always. It wasn't foolproof. I wasn't Zeus. There were no magic thunderbolts at my disposal. But it is nice to build up, over the years, things that you know do — on occasion — work. Weapons for the war that subsides but that can always ignite again. And so writing, reading, talking, travelling, yoga, meditation and running were some of mine.

The brain is the body —part two

I believe that the term 'mental illness' is misleading, as it implies all the problems that happen, happen above the neck. With depression, and with anxiety in particular, a lot of the problems may be generated by the mind, and aggravate the mind, but have physical effects.

For instance, the NHS website lists these as the psychological symptoms of generalised anxiety disorder:

restlessness
a sense of dread
feeling constantly 'on edge'
difficulty concentrating
irritability
impatience
being easily distracted

But interestingly the NHS gives a much longer list for the physical symptoms:

dizziness
drowsiness and tiredness
pins and needles

irregular heartbeat (palpitations)
muscle aches and tension
dry mouth
excessive sweating
shortness of breath
stomach ache
nausea
diarrhoea
headache
excessive thirst
frequent urinating
painful or missed periods
difficulty falling or staying asleep (insomnia)

One symptom missing from the NHS list, but found on others, is both physical and mental. *Derealisation*. It is a very real symptom that makes you feel, well, *not real*. You don't feel fully inside yourself. You feel like you are controlling your body from somewhere else. It is like the distance between a writer and their fictional, semi-autobiographical narrator. The centre that is you has gone. It is a feeling of the mind and the body, once again proving to the sufferer that to separate the two as crudely as we do is wrong, and simplistic. And maybe even part of the problem.

Famous people

Depression makes you feel alone. That's one of its main symptoms. So it helps to know you are not alone. Given the nature of our society, and a confessional celebrity culture, it is often famous people that we hear about having troubles. But it doesn't matter. The more we hear, the better. Well, not always. Being a writer, I don't particularly like thinking about Ernest Hemingway and what he did with his gun, or Sylvia Plath's head in her oven. I didn't even like contemplating too deeply non-writer Vincent Van Gogh and his ear. And when I heard about a contemporary writer I admired, David Foster Wallace, hanging himself on 12 September 2008 it actually sparked in me my worst bout of depression since the really Bad Times. And it doesn't have to be writers. I was one of millions of people not just saddened by Robin Williams' death, but scared of it, as if it somehow made it more likely for us to end up the same way.

But then, most people with depression — even most famous people with depression — don't end up committing suicide. Mark Twain suffered depression and died of a heart attack.

Tennessee Williams died from accidentally choking on the cap of a bottle of eye drops that he frequently used.

Sometimes just looking at names of people who have suffered depression — or are still suffering depression — but who clearly have (or had) other things that are great going on in their lives, gives a kind of comfort. So here is my list:

Buzz Aldrin
Halle Berry
Zach Braff
Russell Brand
Frank Bruno
Alastair Campbell
Jim Carrey
Winston Churchill
Richard Dreyfuss
Carrie Fisher
F. Scott Fitzgerald
Stephen Fry
Judy Garland
Jon Hamm
Anne Hathaway
Billy Joel
Angelina Jolie
Stephen King
Abraham Lincoln
Wolfgang Amadeus Mozart

Isaac Newton
Al Pacino
Gwyneth Paltrow
Dolly Parton
Princess Diana
Christina Ricci
Teddy Roosevelt
Winona Ryder
Brooke Shields
Charles Shulz
Ben Stiller
William Styron
Emma Thompson
Uma Thurman
Marcus Trescothick
Ruby Wax
Robbie Williams
Tennessee Williams
Catherine Zeta-Jones

And what does this teach us? That depression can happen to prime ministers and presidents and cricketers and playwrights and boxers and the stars of hit Hollywood comedies. Well, we knew that. What else? That fame and money do not immunise you from mental health problems. We kind of knew that too. Maybe it is not about teaching us anything except that knowing about Jim Carrey's time on Prozac or Princess Leia's bipolar disorder helps us because, while we know it can happen to anyone, we can never be told too many times that *it can actually happen to anyone*.

I remember sitting in a dentist's reading an interview with Halle Berry in which she was talking openly about the time she sat in her car, in a garage, and tried to kill herself via carbon monoxide poisoning. She told the interviewer that the only thing that stopped her was the thought of her mother finding her.

It helped me, seeing her smiling and looking strong in that magazine. It may have been a Photoshopped illusion, but whatever, she was alive and seemingly happy, and a member of the same species as me. So yes, we like stories of recovery. We love the narrative structure of rise-fall-rise-again. Celebrity magazines run these stories endlessly.

There is a lot of cynicism about depressed celebrities, as if after a certain amount of success and money a human being becomes immune to mental illnesses. It is only mental illnesses that people seem to say this about. They don't say it about the flu, for instance. Unlike a book or a film depression doesn't have to be *about* something.

Also, one of the things depression often does is make you feel guilt. Depression says

'Look at you, with your nice life, with your nice boyfriend/girlfriend/husband/wife/kids/dog/sofa/Twitter followers, with your good job, with your lack of physical health problems, with your holiday in Rome to look forward to, with your mortgage nearly paid off, with your non-divorced parents, with your whatever,' on and on and on.

Actually, depression can be exacerbated by things being all right externally, because the gulf between what you are feeling and what you are *expected* to feel becomes larger. If you feel the same amount of depression as someone would naturally feel in a prisoner of war camp, but you are not in a prisoner of war camp, and are instead in a nice semi-detached house in the free world, then you think 'Crap, this is everything I ever wanted, why aren't I happy?'

You may find yourself, as in the Talking Heads song, in a beautiful house, with a beautiful wife, wondering how you got there. Watching the days. Wondering how things get on top. Wondering what is missing. Wondering if every thing we have wanted in our lives has been the wrong thing. Wondering if the smartphones and nice bathrooms and state-of-the-art TVs we thought were part of the solution are part of the problem. Wondering if, in the board game of life, everything we thought was a ladder was in fact a snake, sliding us right down to the bottom. As any Buddhist would tell you, an over-attachment to material things will lead only to more suffering.

It is said that insanity is a logical response to an insane world. Maybe depression is in part simply a response to a life we don't really understand. Of course, no one understands their life completely if they think about it. An annoying thing about depression is that thinking about life is inevitable. Depression makes thinkers out of all of us. Just ask Abraham Lincoln.

Abraham Lincoln and the
fearful gift

Abraham Lincoln, when he was thirty-two, declared: 'I am now the most miserable man living.' He had, by that age, experienced two massive depressive breakdowns.

'If what I feel were equally distributed to the whole human family, there would not be one cheerful face on the earth. Whether I shall ever be better I can not tell; I awfully forbode I shall not. To remain as I am is impossible. I must die or be better.'

Yet, of course, while Lincoln openly declared he had no fear of suicide, he did not kill himself. He chose to live.

There is a great article on 'Lincoln's Great Depression' in *The Atlantic* by Joshua Wolf Shenk. In it, Shenk writes of how depression forced Lincoln into a deeper understanding of life:

He insisted on acknowledging his fears. Through his late twenties and early thirties he drove deeper and deeper into them, hovering over what, according to

Albert Camus, is the only serious question human beings have to deal with. He asked whether he could live, whether he could face life's misery. Finally he decided that he must . . . He had an 'irrepressible desire' to accomplish something while he lived.

He was evidently a serious person. One of the great serious people of history. He fought mental wars and physical ones. Maybe his knowledge of suffering led to the kind of empathy he showed when seeking to change the law on slavery. ('Wherever I hear anyone arguing for slavery, I feel a strong impulse to see it tried on him personally,' he said.)

Lincoln is not the only famous leader to have battled depression. Winston Churchill lived with the 'black dog' for much of his life too. Watching a fire, he once remarked to a young researcher he was employing: 'I know why logs spit. I know what it is to be consumed.'

Indeed he did. He was — in terms of career achievements — one of the most active men who ever lived. Yet he continually felt despondent and full of darkness.

The political philosopher John Gray — one of my favourite non-fiction writers (read *Straw Dogs* to see why) — believes Churchill didn't 'overcome' depression to become a good war leader, rather that the experience of depression directly enabled him to be one.

Gray argues, in an article for the BBC, that it was Churchill's 'exceptional openness' to intense emotion that explains how he was able to sense dangers that more conventional minds failed to see. 'For most of the politicians and opinion-makers who wanted to appease Hitler, the Nazis were not much more than a raucous expression of German nationalism,' writes Gray. It needed an unusual mind to address an unusual threat. 'He owed his foresight of the horror that was to come to visits of the black dog.'

So, yes, depression is a nightmare. But can it also be a useful one? Can it be one that improves the world in various ways?

Sometimes the links between depression, anxiety and productivity are undeniable. Think of Edvard Munch's omnipresent painting *The Scream*, for instance. Not only is this a most accurate visual depiction of what a panic attack feels like, but it was also — according to the artist himself — directly inspired by a moment of existential terror. Here is the diary entry:

I was walking down the road when the sun set; suddenly, the sky turned as red as blood. I stopped and leaned against the fence, feeling unspeakably tired. Tongues of fire and blood stretched over the bluish black fjord. My friends went on walking, while I lagged behind, shivering with fear. Then I heard the enormous, infinite scream of nature.

But even without the 'smoking gun' of a specific depressive episode inspiring a specific work of genius, it is impossible to ignore the sheer number of greats who have battled depression. Even without focusing on the Plaths and Hemingways and Woolfs who actually killed themselves, the list of known depressives is staggering. And many times there is a link between the illness and the work they produce.

A lot of Freud's work was based on his analysis of his own depression, and what he believed to be the solution. Cocaine was what worked for him, but then — after dishing it out to other sufferers — he started to realise it could be a tad addictive.

Franz Kafka is another member of the Depression Hall of Fame. He suffered from social anxiety and what people now see as clinical depression all his life. He was also a hypochondriac living in fear of physical and mental change. But being a hypochondriac doesn't mean you won't get ill, and when he was thirty-four Kafka contracted tuberculosis. Interestingly, all the things that were known to help Kafka's depression — swimming, horse riding, hiking — were physically healthy pursuits.

Surely the claustrophobia and sense of powerlessness in his works — so often interpreted in solely political terms — was also a result of him suffering from an illness that makes you feel claustrophobic?

Kafka's most famous story is *The Metamorphosis*. A travelling salesman wakes up to find himself transformed into a giant insect, who has overslept and is late for work. It is a story about the dehumanising effect of capitalism, yes, but it can equally be read as a metaphor for depression, the most Kafkaesque of illnesses. For, like Gregor Samsa, the depressive can sometimes wake up in the room they fell asleep in, and yet feel totally different. An alien to themselves. Trapped in a nightmare.

Likewise, could Emily Dickinson have written her poem 'I felt a Funeral, in my Brain' without deep mental anguish? Of course, most depressives don't end up being a Lincoln or a Dickinson or a Churchill or a Munch or a Freud or a Kafka (or a Mark Twain or a Sylvia Plath or a Georgia O'Keeffe or an Ian

161

Curtis or a Kurt Cobain). But then, nor do most people.

People often use the word 'despite' in the context of mental illness. So-and-so did such-and-such *despite* having depression/anxiety/OCD/agoraphobia/whatever. But sometimes that 'despite' should be a 'because'. For instance, I write because of depression. I was not a writer before. The intensity needed — to explore things with relentless curiosity and energy — simply wasn't there. Fear makes us curious. Sadness makes us philosophise. ('To be or not to be?' is a daily question for many depressives.)

Going back to Abraham Lincoln, the key thing to note is that the president always suffered with depression. He never fully overcame it, but he lived alongside it and achieved great things. 'Whatever greatness Lincoln achieved cannot be explained as a triumph over personal suffering,' says Joshua Wolf Shenk in that article I mentioned. 'Rather, it must be accounted an outgrowth of the same system that produced that suffering . . . Lincoln didn't do great work because he solved the problem of his melancholy; the problem of his melancholy was all the more fuel for the fire of his great work.'

So. Even if depression is not totally

overcome, we can learn to use what the poet Byron called a 'fearful gift'.

We don't have to use it to rule a nation, like Churchill or Lincoln. We don't even have to use it to paint a really good picture.

We can just use it in life. For instance, I find that being grimly aware of mortality can make me steadfastly determined to enjoy life where life can be enjoyed. It makes me value precious moments with my children, and with the woman I love. It adds intensity in bad ways, but also good ways.

Art and political vigour are just one spill-over of that intensity, but it can manifest itself in a million other ways, most of which won't make you famous but many of which will, in the long term, add as well as take away.

Depression is . . .

An internal war.
A black dog (thanks, Winston Churchill and Dr Johnson).
A black hole.
An invisible fire.
A pressure cooker.
A devil inside.
A prison.
An absence.
A bell jar ('I would be sitting under the same glass bell jar,' wrote Plath, 'stewing in my own sour air').
A malicious code in the operating system of your mind.
A parallel universe.
A life-long fight.
A by-product of mortality.
A living nightmare.
An echo chamber.
Dark and hopeless and lonely.
A collision between an ancient mind and a modern world (evolutionary psychology).
A fucking pain.

Depression is also . . .

Smaller than you.

Always, it is smaller than you, even when it feels vast. It operates within you, you do not operate within it. It may be a dark cloud passing across the sky, but — if that is the metaphor — you are the sky.

You were there before it. And the cloud can't exist without the sky, but the sky can exist without the cloud.

A conversation across time — part three

THEN ME: It's terrifying.

NOW ME: What is?

THEN ME: Life. My mind. The weight of it.

NOW ME: Shhh. Stop that. You are just a bit trapped inside a moment. The moment will change.

THEN ME: Andrea will leave me.

NOW ME: No. No, she won't. She'll marry you.

THEN ME: Ha! As if anyone would tie themselves to a useless freak like me. Would they?

NOW ME: Yes. And look, you are making progress. You go to the shop now and you don't have a panic attack. You don't feel that weight on you all the time.

THEN ME: I do.

NOW ME: No. There was that time last week when I — when *you* — were out in the sunshine walking through the park, and you felt a lightness. A moment you weren't really thinking.

THEN ME: Actually, yes. Yes. That's true. I had another this morning. I was lying in bed just wondering if we had any cereal left. That was it. It was just a normal thing, and it lasted over a minute. Just lying there, thinking about breakfast.

NOW ME: *See?* So you know things aren't always going to be the same. I mean, things *today* weren't always the same.

THEN ME: But it's still so intense.

NOW ME: And it always will be. You will always be quite intense. And the depression might always be there, waiting for the next fall. But there is so much *life* waiting for you. The one thing depression has told you is that a day can be a long and intense stretch of time.

THEN ME: Oh God, yes.

NOW ME: Well, then, don't worry about the passing of time. There can be infinity inside a day.

THEN ME: I could be bounded in a nutshell and count myself a king of infinite space.

NOW ME: Hamlet? Impressive. I've forgotten all those lines by now. It's been a long time since university.

THEN ME: I am starting to believe in you.

NOW ME: Thank you.

THEN ME: I mean, the possibility of you. The possibility that I exist more than a decade in the future. And that I feel a lot better.

NOW ME: It's true. You do. And you have a family of your own. You have a life. It is not perfect. No human life is. But it is yours.

THEN ME: I want proof.

NOW ME: I can't prove it. There is no time machine.

THEN ME: No. I suppose I'll just have to hope.

NOW ME: Yes. Have faith.

THEN ME: I'll try.

NOW ME: You already have.

4
Living

'And thus the heart will break, yet brokenly
live on'
        — Lord Byron, *Childe Harold's Pilgrimage*

The world

The world is increasingly designed to depress us. Happiness isn't very good for the economy. If we were happy with what we had, why would we need more? How do you sell an anti-ageing moisturiser? You make someone worry about ageing. How do you get people to vote for a political party? You make them worry about immigration. How do you get them to buy insurance? By making them worry about everything. How do you get them to have plastic surgery? By highlighting their physical flaws. How do you get them to watch a TV show? By making them worry about missing out. How do you get them to buy a new smartphone? By making them feel like they are being left behind.

To be calm becomes a kind of revolutionary act. To be happy with your own non-upgraded existence. To be comfortable with our messy, human selves, would not be good for business.

Yet we have no other world to live in. And actually, when we really look closely, the world of stuff and advertising is not really life. Life is the other stuff. Life is what is left when you take all that crap away, or at least ignore it for a while.

Life is the people who love you. No one will ever choose to stay alive for an iPhone. It's the people we reach via the iPhone that matter.

And once we begin to recover, and to live again, we do so with new eyes. Things become clearer, and we are aware of things we weren't aware of before.

Mushroom clouds

I never saw the double-whammy of anxiety and depression coming before it knocked me out when I was twenty-four. But I should have done. The warning signs were all there. The moments of despair as a teenager. The continual worrying about everything. In particular, I believe there were also a lot warning signs while I was a student at Hull University. The trouble with warning signs, though, is that we only have the past to go on, not the future, and if something hasn't actually happened it is hard to know that it will.

The advantage of having *had* depression is that you know what to look for, and there was plenty to spot while I was at uni, but I never noticed it.

I used to stare into space, while sitting on the fifth floor of the university library, imagining, with a kind of bleak terror, mushroom clouds on the horizon. I used to feel slightly strange sometimes. Blurred around the edges, as if I was a walking watercolour. And I did need to drink a lot of alcohol, now I think about it.

I also had what was a panic attack, though not on the scale of the later ones. Here is what happened.

As part of my joint English–History degree I took a module on Art History. Though I didn't realise it at the time, that meant that at some point in the term I would have to do a presentation on a modern art movement (I chose Cubism).

It sounds like nothing, but I was dreading it as much as you could dread anything. I had always been scared of performing and public speaking. But this was something else. I simply could not come to terms with the idea that I would have to stand in front of an entire seminar room full of — ooh — twelve, maybe thirteen people, and talk to them for twenty minutes. People who would be actively thinking about me and concentrating on me and listening to the words coming out of my mouth.

'Everyone gets nervous,' my mum told me, on the phone. 'It's nothing. And the closer you get to it, the closer it is to being over.'

But what did she know?

I mean, what if I got a nosebleed? What if I couldn't speak at all? What if I pissed myself? There were other doubts too. How do you say Picabia? Should I use a French accent for the name of Georges Braque's painting *Nature morte?*

For about five weeks I couldn't really enjoy anything because this was coming up, and I couldn't do a no-show because it was assessed, as part of coursework. The thing that I was particularly worried about was the fact that I had to co-ordinate reading my words with the presenting of slides. What if I put the slides in upside down? What if I spoke about Juan Gris' *Portrait of Picasso* while actually showing a Picasso? There were a seemingly infinite number of nightmare possibilities.

Fittingly, given the subject of the talk was an art movement that involved abandoning perspective, I was losing perspective.

The day came. Tuesday, 17 March 1997. It looked like so many other drab Hull days. But it wasn't. Looks were deceptive. There was threat in the air. Everything — even the furniture in our student house — looked like secret weapons in an invisible war against me. Reading *Dracula* for my Gothic Literature module wasn't helping either. ('I am all in a sea of wonders. I doubt; I fear; I think strange things, which I dare not confess to my own soul.')

'You could always pretend to be ill,' my new girlfriend and future wife Andrea said.

'No, I can't. It's assessed. It's *assessed*!'

'Jesus, Matt, calm down. You have turned

this into something it's not.'

And then I went to the chemist and bought a pack of Natracalm and swallowed as many of the twenty-four tablets as I could manage. (I think about sixteen. Two sheets' worth. They tasted of grass and chalk.) I waited to feel the calm that was promised.

But it didn't happen. Itching happened. And then a rash happened.

The rash was all over my neck and hands. Angry red blotches. My skin felt not only immensely itchy but also hot. The seminar wasn't until quarter past two. Maybe the rash was a stress response. Maybe I needed something else to calm me down. I went to the union bar and had a pint of lager and two vodka and limes. I had a cigarette. With ten minutes to go before the presentation was due to begin I was in the toilets in the History Department, staring at a swastika some idiot had biro'd onto the shining blonde wood of the door.

My neck was getting worse. I stayed in the toilets. Silently briefing myself in the mirror.

I felt the power of time. The power of it as something unmoving.

'Stop,' I whispered. But time doesn't stop. Not even when you ask it nicely.

Then I did it. I did the presentation. I stuttered and sounded frail as an autumn leaf in my head and messed up the slides a couple of times and failed to say anything at all that I didn't have written down in front of me in my best handwriting. People didn't giggle at my rash. They just looked deeply, deeply uncomfortable.

But halfway through I became detached from myself. I *derealised*. The string that holds on to that feeling of selfhood, the feeling of being me, was cut, and it floated away like a helium balloon. I suppose it was your standard out-of-body experience. I was there, not exactly above myself, but above and beside and everywhere all at once, watching and hearing myself in a state of such heightened self-consciousness I'd actually burst right out of myself altogether.

It was, I suppose, a panic attack. My first actual proper one, though nowhere near the scale of those I'd know later in Ibiza, or back living at home with my parents. It should have been a warning sign, but it wasn't, because I had been panicking *for a reason*. Okay, so it wasn't much of one, but in my head it was. And if you are having a panic attack for a reason — a lion is chasing you, the lift door won't open, you don't know how to pronounce 'chiaroscuro' — then it is not really a panic attack, but a logical response to a fearful situation.

To panic without a reason, that's madness. To panic with a reason, that's sanity. I was still on the right side of the line.

Just.

But it is always hard for us to see the future inside the present, even when it is right there in front of us.

The Big A

Anxiety is the partner of depression. It accompanies half the cases of depression. Sometimes it triggers depression. Sometimes depression triggers anxiety. Sometimes they simply co-exist, like a nightmare marriage. Though of course it is perfectly possible to have anxiety minus depression, and vice versa.

Anxiety and depression are an interesting mix. In many ways they are opposite experiences, and yet mix them together and you don't get a happy medium. Quite the opposite. Anxiety, which often bubbles up into panic, is a nightmare in fast-forward. Anxiety, even more than depression, can be exacerbated by the way we live in the twenty-first century. By the things that surround us.

Smartphones. Advertising (I think of a great David Foster Wallace line — 'It did what all ads are supposed to do: create an anxiety relievable by purchase.') Twitter followers. Facebook likes. Instagram. Information overload. Unanswered emails. Dating apps. War. The rapid evolution of technology. Urban planning. The changing climate. Overcrowded public transport. Articles on the 'post-antibiotic age'. Photoshopped cover models. Google-induced hypochondria. Infinite choice ('anxiety is the dizziness of freedom' — Søren Kierkegaard). Online shopping. The should-we-eat-butter? debate. Atomised living. All those American TV dramas we should have watched. All those prize-winning books we should have read. All those pop stars we haven't heard of. All that *lacking* we are made to feel. Instant gratification. Constant distraction. Work work work. Twenty-four-hour everything.

Maybe to be truly in tune with the modern world means anxiety is inevitable. But here we must again distinguish between anxiety and 'Anxiety'. For instance, I was always an anxious person. As a child I used to worry about death a lot. Certainly more than a child should. I also used to climb into my parents' bed as a ten-year-old and tell them I was too scared to go to sleep in case I woke up without the ability to see or hear. I used to worry about meeting new people, I'd get stomach aches on Sunday nights about Monday mornings, I even cried once — when I was fourteen — about the fact that music wasn't as good as it had been when I was little. I was a sensitive child, it's fair to say.

But Anxiety proper — generalised anxiety disorder and the related panic disorder that I was diagnosed with too — can be (but isn't always) a desperate thing. It can be a full-time occupation of gale-force worry.

That said, from my personal experience, anxiety — even more than depression — is very treatable.

Slow down

If you suffer from anxiety on its own, or the fast-speed kind of depression that comes when it is fused with anxiety, there are things you can do. Some people take pills. For some they are a literal lifesaver. But as we've seen, finding the right pill is a tricky science because, in truth, the science of the brain is itself *not quite there*.

The tools used to analyse the processes of living human brains — things like CAT (computed axial tomography) scans and, later, MRI (magnetic resonance imaging) scans have only been in existence a few decades. Of course, these things are very good at providing pretty, multi-coloured pictures of the brain, and telling us which parts of the brain are most active. They can point to things like the part of the brain responsible for the pleasurable feeling we get when we eat a chocolate bar, or for the distress when we hear a baby cry. Clever stuff. But there are weaknesses.

'Most parts of the brain do different things at different times,' says Dr David Adam, author of *The Man Who Couldn't Stop*. 'The amygdala, for example, plays a role in both sexual arousal and terror — but an MRI scan cannot differentiate between passion and panic . . . So what should we think when the amygdala lights up on an MRI scan when we are shown a picture of Cameron Diaz or Brad Pitt — that we are afraid of them?'

So, the tools aren't perfect. And neuroscience isn't perfect.

Some things are known, but more isn't. Maybe this lack of true understanding explains why there is still stigma about mental health. Where there is mystery, there will be fear.

Ultimately, there remains no sure-fire cure. There are pills, but only a liar would say they work every time or that they are always an ideal solution. It is also rare that they cure someone without additional help. But when it comes to the anxiety side at least, there does seem to be one thing that works across the board, to a greater or lesser degree.

Namely: *slowing down*. Anxiety runs your mind at fast-forward rather than normal 'play' speed, so addressing that issue of mental 'pace' might not be easy. But it works. Anxiety takes away all the commas and full stops we need to make sense of ourselves.

Here are some ways to add back that mental punctuation:

Yoga. I was a yogaphobe, but am now a convert. It's great, because unlike other therapies, it treats the mind and the body as part of the same whole.

Slow your breathing. Not crazy deep breaths. Just gentle. In for five, out for five. It's hard to stick to, but it is very hard for panic to happen if your breathing is relaxed. So many anxiety symptoms — dizziness, pins and needles, tingling — are directly related to shallow breathing.

Meditate. You don't have to chant. Just sit down for five minutes and try and think of a single calming thing. A boat moored in a glittering sea. The face of someone you love. Or just focus on your breathing.

Accept. Don't fight things, feel them. Tension is about opposition, relaxation is about letting go.

Live in the present. Here is meditation master Amit Ray: 'If you want to conquer the anxiety of life, live in the moment. Live in the breath.'

Love. Anaïs Nin called anxiety 'love's greatest killer'. But fortunately, the reverse is also true. Love is anxiety's greatest killer. Love is an outward force. It is our road out of our own terrors, because anxiety is an illness that wraps us up in our own nightmares. This is not selfishness, even though people read it as such. If your leg is on fire, it is not selfish to concentrate on the pain, or the fear of the flames. So it is with anxiety. People with mental illnesses aren't wrapped up in themselves because they are intrinsically any more selfish than other people. Of course not. They are just feeling things that can't be ignored. Things that point the arrows inward. But having people who love you and who you love is such a help. This doesn't have to be romantic, or even familial love. Forcing yourself to see the world through love's gaze can be healthy. Love is an attitude to life. It can save us.

Peaks and troughs

As I have said, whenever I panicked I wished for a real danger. If you are having a panic attack for a reason then it is not really a panic attack, but a logical response to a fearful situation. Likewise, whenever I felt that downward gearshift towards that heavy and infinite sadness, I wished it had an external cause.

But, as time grew on, I knew something I hadn't known earlier. I knew that down wasn't the only direction. If you hung in there, if you stuck it out, then things got better. They get better and then they get worse and then they get better.

Peaks and troughs, peaks and troughs, as a homeopath had told me, while I was living at my parents' house (the homeopath's words had worked better than her tinctures).

Parenthesis

(It's a weird thing, depression. Even now, writing this with a good distance of fourteen years from my lowest point, I haven't fully escaped. You get over it, but at the same time you never get over it. It comes back in flashes, when you are tired or anxious or have been eating the wrong stuff, and catches you off guard. I woke up with it a few days ago, in fact. I felt its dark wisps around my head, that ominous life-is-fear feeling. But then, after a morning with the best five- and six-year-olds in the world, it subsided. It is now an aside. Something to put brackets around. Life lesson: the way out is never through yourself.)

Parties

For ten years of my life I could not go to a party without being terrified. Yes, here was me, who had worked in Ibiza for the largest and wildest weekly party in Europe, unable to step into a room full of happy people holding wine glasses without having a panic attack.

Shortly after I became published, and was worried that I would soon be dropped, I felt obliged to attend a literary Christmas party. I was sober, as I was still petrified of alcohol, and I headed into a room and instantly felt out of my depth as famous brainy people (Zadie Smith, David Baddiel, Graham Swift) seemed to be everywhere, with their famous brainy faces, totally in their element.

Of course, it is never easy walking into a room full of people. There is that awkward moment of hovering around, like a serious lonely molecule, while everyone else is in their tight little circles, all laughter and conversation.

I stood in the middle of the room, looking for someone I knew for reasons other than that they were famous, and couldn't see anyone. I held my glass of sparkling mineral water (I was too scared of caffeine and sugar to have anything else) and tried to think my discomfort made me a genius. After all, Keats and Beethoven and Charlotte Brontë hated parties. But then I realised there were probably millions of historical non-geniuses who also hated them too.

For a couple of seconds, I kind of accidentally locked eyes with Zadie Smith. She turned away. She was clearly thinking I was a weirdo. *The Queen of Literature thinks I am a weirdo!*

One hundred and ninety-one years before this party, and only a couple of miles away, Keats had sat down to write a letter to his friend Richard Woodhouse.

'When I am in a room with People,' he wrote, 'if I ever am free from speculating on creations of my own brain, then not myself goes home to myself: but the identity of every one in the room begins to press upon me so that I am in a very little time annihilated.'

As I stood there, and those bubbles of carbon dioxide rose in my glass, I felt a kind of annihilation. I began to be not entirely sure I was there at all, and I felt floaty. This was it. A relapse. Weeks, maybe months, of depression awaited me.

Breathe, I told myself. *Just breathe.*

I needed Andrea. The air was getting

thinner. I was in the zone. I had passed the event horizon. It was no good. I was lost in a black hole of my own making.

I put my glass down on a table and got out of there. I left a coat in the cloakroom that could still be there for all I know. I stepped into the London night and ran back the short distance to the café where Andrea, my eternal saviour, waited for me.

'What's the matter?' she asked. 'I thought you were going to be an hour?'

'I couldn't. I needed to get out of there.'

'Well, you are out. How do you feel?'

I thought about this. How did I feel? Like an idiot, obviously. But also, my panic attack had gone. In the old days, my panic attacks didn't just go. They simply morphed into more panic attacks, breaking me down, like an army, until depression could come in and colonise my head. But no. I was feeling quite normal again. A normal person who was allergic to parties. I had wanted to die in the party, but not literally. Really, I had just wanted to escape the room. But I at least had walked into the room in the first place. That itself was progress. A year later I would be better enough to not only go to the party, but to travel there on my own. Sometimes on the rocky, windy path of recovery, what feels like failure can be a step forward.

#reasonstostayalive

I asked some people online who have experience of depression, anxiety or suicidal thoughts, 'What keeps you going?' These were their reasons to stay alive:

@Matineegirl
Friends, family, acceptance, sharing, knowing the black dog will leave eventually. #reasonstostayalive

@mannyliz
Very simply my children. They didn't ask to be born to a mum who at times struggles to keep it together.

@groznez
#reasonstostayalive Yoga. Couldn't be without it.

@Ginny–Bradwell
#reasonstostayalive Realising it was ok to be ill and that there were no quick fixes.

@AlRedboots
The hole you'd leave is bigger than the pain

you suffer by being. #reasonstostayalive

@LeeJamesHarrison
To spite yourself for those intermittent spiteless days and moments that are HD quality wonderful as a result.

@H3llInHighH33ls
There are moments and days when the fog lifts. Those times are glorious. #reasonstostayalive

@simone–mc
My #reasonstostayalive? The future. The undiscovered country. To find and meet other people who appreciate corny Star Trek references.

@Erastes
#reasonstostayalive The days start lengthening after December 21. Something to cling to in the dark times.

@PixleTVPi
My only reason to stay alive is my best friend. #reasonstostayalive

@paperbookmarks
because even though I'm in constant pain, I have the most supportive people around me, and the best books to read. #reasonstostay-alive

@ameliasnelling
#reasonstostayalive I still haven't seen Iceland where my ashes will be scattered.

@debecca
#reasonstostayalive To spite cancer, Bipolar and all the other things trying to kill me young.

@vivatrampv
The surgeons worked so hard to give me the future that I deserve to have. #reasonstostayalive

@lillianharpl
#reasonstostayalive Since the other option isn't flexible.

@NickiDavies
I'm weird, an optimistic depressive! Even when it's really bad I still believe it can be better. #reasonstostayalive

@Leilah–Makes
I'm comforted by maintaining habits. It allows me a little control. #reasonstostayalive

@Doc–Megz–to–be
The uncertain future. It may cause anxiety but it is also like a book that is really hard to predict. #reasonstostayalive

@ilonacatherine
Not everyone thinks you're as much of a waste of space as you do when in the depths of depression. Trust others. #reasonstostayalive

@stueygod
Music. #reasonstostayalive

@ameliasward
Sunny mornings. #reasonstostayalive

@DolinaMunro
Bacon rolls. #reasonstostayalive

@mirandafay
Fresh air. The uncompromising love of a good dog. #reasonstostayalive

@jeebreslin
Because inside there is a golden you who loves you and wants you to win and prevail and be happy. #reasonstostayalive

@ylovesgok
The realisation I can get help. #reasonstostayalive

@wilsonxox
Sunsets. And that particularly unspecific

musical genre with access to your spine. #reasonstostayalive

@MagsTheObscure
The brother I look after. This is one of the main reasons I remain a carer. He's my lighthouse in the storm. #reasons-tostayalive

@jaras76
Possibilities. Overcoming the next challenge. Soccer. #reasonstostayalive

@HHDreamWolf
Suicide may lead to my friends and family becoming depressed, I would never wish depression on anyone. #reasonstostayalive

@DebWonda
Everything passes — joy follows pain, warmth melts the ice. #reasonstostayalive

@legallyogi
My last depression was a severe post-natal. It was an awful time. My #reasonstostayalive were my family and knowing it would pass.

@ayaanidilsays
#reasonstostayalive I'd say best friends. The Great Perhaps.

@lordofl
The dogs always need walking in the morning. #reasons-tostayalive

@UTBookblog
The experience to know that tomorrow will be a better day. My family, boyfriend, friends . . . and my TBR pile! #reasonstostayalive

@GoodWithoutGods
#reasonstostayalive Because 7×10^{49} atoms won't arrange themselves this way ever again. It's a one-off privilege.

@Book–Geek–Says
The support of my mum and now my boyfriend who got together with me at one of my lowest points three years ago. #reasons-tostayalive

@Teens22
#reasonstostayalive Love is the best reason to stay alive. Self-love, love for other people, love of life and noticing the good. #reasonstostay-alive

@ZODIDOG
#reasonstostayalive Some days it's as simple as blue skies & sunshine. Or the cuteness and reward from my pet chinchilla.

@Halftongue
Sometimes my #reasonstostayalive amount to no more than 'people would be sad and angry if I didn't.' Those are bad days.

@tara818
#reasonstostayalive I had to feed my baby. I had crippling anxiety & post-natal depression, only here because of having to nurse him.

@BeverlyBambury
Don't always know why I kept moving, but it never — for long — felt like an option not to. Grim determination? #reasonstostayalive

@wolri
#reasonstostayalive Simple things — husband's support, not crowding me when I'm having a bad time, mainly my family & my little dog.

@Lyssa–1234
Not wanting to hurt parents/sibling/partner. No matter how low I get, I know that these people would miss me. #reasonstostayalive

@BlondeBookGirl
My #reasonstostayalive include 'picturing my cat's little face if I wasn't here', 'my

mum/sister' and 'all the books I really want to read.'

@gourenina
Knowing my depression has never lasted forever, and there has always been a way out. #reasonstostayalive

@Despard
It's been better before and it will be again. #reasonstostayalive

Things that make me worse

Coffee.
Lack of sleep.
The dark.
The cold.
September.
October.
Mid-afternoons.
Tight muscles.
The pace of contemporary existence.
Bad posture.
Being away from the people I love.
Sitting for too long.
Advertising.
Feeling ignored.
Waking up at three in the morning.
TV.
Bananas (I am not sure about this one, it is
   probably a coincidence).
Alcohol.
Facebook (sometimes).
Twitter (sometimes).
Deadlines.
Editing.
Difficult decisions (you know, which socks to
   wear).

Getting physically ill.
Thinking I am feeling depressed (the most vicious of circles).
Not drinking enough water.
Checking my Amazon ranking.
Checking other writers' Amazon rankings.
Walking into a social function on my own.
Train travel.
Hotel rooms.
Being alone.

Things that (sometimes) make me better

Mindfulness.
Running.
Yoga.
Summer.
Sleep.
Slow breathing.
Being around people I love.
Reading Emily Dickinson poems.
Reading some of Graham Greene's *The Power and the Glory*.
Writing.
Eating well.
Long baths/showers.
Eighties movies.
Listening to music.
Facebook (sometimes).
Twitter (sometimes).
Going for a long walk.
'Noble deeds and hot baths' (Dodie Smith).
Making burritos.
Light skies and walls.
Reading Keats' letters. ('Do you not see how necessary a world of pains and troubles is to school an intelligence and make it a soul?')

The bank of bad days.

Large rooms.

Doing something selfless.

The smell of bread.

Wearing clean clothes (come on, I'm a writer, this is rarer than you'd think).

Thinking I have things that work for me.

Knowing that other things work for other people.

Absorbing myself into something.

Knowing that someone else may read these words and that, just maybe, the pain I felt wasn't for nothing.

5
Being

'Put your ear down next to your soul and listen hard.'

— Anne Sexton

In praise of thin skins

I have a thin skin.

I think this is part and parcel of depression and anxiety, or — to be precise — being a person quite likely to get depression and anxiety. I also think that I will never fully get over my breakdown fourteen years ago. If the stone falls hard enough the ripples last a lifetime.

I have gone from never feeling happy to feeling happy — or at last somewhere in the ballpark — most of the time. So I am lucky. But I have blips. Either blips when I am genuinely depressed/anxious or blips caused by me fighting the onset of depression/anxiety by doing something stupid (getting excessively drunk and coming home at five in the morning after losing my wallet and having to plead with taxi drivers to take me home). But generally, day to day, I don't fight it. I accept things more. This is who I am. And besides, *fighting* it actually makes it worse. The trick is to befriend depression and anxiety. To be thankful for them, because then you can deal with them a whole lot better. And the way I have befriended them is by thanking them for my thin skin.

Sure, without a thin skin I would have never known those terrible days of nothingness. Those days of either panic, or intense, bone-scorching lethargy. The days of self-hate, or drowning under invisible waves. I sometimes felt, in my self-pity, too fragile for a world of speed and right angles and noise. (I love Jonathan Rottenberg's evolutionary theory of depression, that it is to do with being unable to adapt to the present: 'An ancient mood system has collided with a highly novel operating environment created by a remarkable species.')

But would I go along to a magical mind spa and ask for a skin-thickening treatment? Probably not. You need to feel life's terror to feel its wonder.

And I feel it today, actually, right now, on what could seem like quite a grey, overcast afternoon. I feel the sheer unfathomable marvel that is this strange life we have, here on earth, the seven billion of us, clustered in our towns and cities on this pale blue dot of a planet, spending our allotted 30,000 days as best we can, in glorious insignificance.

I like to feel the force of that miracle. I like to burrow deep into this life, and explore it through the magic of words and the magic of human beings (and the magic of peanut butter sandwiches). And I am glad to feel

210

every tumultuous second of it, and glad for the fact that when I walk into the vast room with all the Tintorettos in it in the National Gallery my skin literally tingles, and my heart palpitates, and I am glad for the synesthesia that means when I read Emily Dickinson or Mark Twain my mind feels actual warmth from those old American words.

Feeling.

That is what it is about.

People place so much value on thought, but feeling is as essential. I want to read books that make me laugh and cry and fear and hope and punch the air in triumph. I want a book to hug me or grab me by the scruff of my neck. I don't even mind if it punches me in the gut. Because we are here to feel.

I want life.

I want to read it and write it and feel it and live it.

I want, for as much of the time as possible in this blink-of-an-eye existence we have, to feel all that can be felt.

I hate depression. I am scared of it. Terrified, in fact. But at the same time, it has made me who I am. And if — for me — it is the price of feeling life, it's a price always worth paying.

I am satisfied just to be.

How to be a bit happier than Schopenhauer

For Arthur Schopenhauer, the depressive's favourite philosopher (and one who influenced Nietzsche, Freud and Einstein in varying but significant ways), life was the pursuit of futile purposes. 'We blow out a soap-bubble as long and as large as possible, although with the perfect certainty that it will burst.' In this view, happiness is impossible, because of all these goals. Goals are the source of misery. An unattained goal causes pain, but actually achieving it brings only a brief satisfaction.

In fact, if you really think about it, a life made of goals is going to be disappointing. Yes, it might propel you forward, keep you turning the pages of your own existence, but ultimately it will leave you empty. Because even if you achieve your goals, what then? You may have gained the thing you lacked, but with it, what then? You either set another goal, stress about how you keep the thing you attained, or you think — along with the millions of people having mid- (or early- or late-) life crises right now — *This is everything I wanted, so why am I not happy?*

So what was Schopenhauer's answer? Well, if wanting things was the problem, the answer had to be in giving things up. In his language, the cause of suffering is intensity of *will*.

Schopenhauer believed that by seeing the bigger picture, by viewing humanity as a whole and its suffering as a whole, a person would turn away from life and deny their instincts. In other words, the Schopenhauer plan involves no sex, very little money, fasting and a fair bit of self-torture.

Only that way — by totally denying human will — can we see the truth that in front of us 'there is certainly only nothingness'.

Bleak, huh?

Well, yes. Although Schopenhauer didn't recommend suicide, he recommended a kind of living suicide, in which anything pleasurable had to be scorned.

But Schopenhauer was a major hypocrite. He talked the talk but couldn't walk the walk. As Bertrand Russell explained in his *History of Western Philosophy*:

He habitually dined well, at a good restaurant, he had many trivial love-affairs, which were sensual but not passionate; he was exceedingly quarrelsome and unusually avaricious. On one occasion he was annoyed by an elderly seamstress who was talking to a friend outside the door of his apartment. He threw her downstairs, causing her permanent injury . . . It is hard to find in his life any virtue except kindness to animals . . . In all other respects he was completely selfish.

Schopenhauer — the ultimate pessimist — actually illustrates how unhappiness works. His work set out anti-goal goals that he couldn't meet.

Now, I don't endorse throwing old women down stairs, but I kind of warm to Schopenhauer. I think he recognised the problem — will, or desire of ego or goal-orientated drive or whichever historical term you want to use — but in life he grappled around in the dark (often literally, given his messy love-life).

So, what's the way out? How do you stop the endless wanting and worrying? How do you get off the treadmill? How do you stop time? How do we stop exhausting ourselves worrying about the future?

★　★　★

The best answers — the answers that have been written and recorded for thousands of years — always seem to resolve around acceptance. Schopenhauer himself was greatly influenced by ancient Eastern philosophy. 'The truth has been recognised by the sages of India,' he said. Indeed, his belief that abstinence from worldly pleasures is the answer to life, is something he shares with a lot of Buddhist thinkers.

But Buddhist thought is not as negative or miserable as Schopenhauer. With Schopenhauer all this asceticism is a bit self-punishing, a bit full of self-loathing, which is unhealthy and counter-productive.

A world full of people hating themselves is not a happy world.

Buddhism does not seem to be about self-punishment.

A key Buddhist symbol is that of the lotus flower. The lotus flower grows in mud at the bottom of a pool, but rises above the murky water and blooms in the clear air, pure and beautiful, before eventually dying. This metaphor for spiritual enlightenment also works as a metaphor for hope and change. The mud you could see as depression or anxiety. The flowers in the clear air, the self we know we can be, unclogged by despair.

Indeed, a lot of the *Dhammapada*, chief among the Buddhist sacred texts (being a record of the Gautama Buddha's teaching), reads like an early self-help book.

'No one saves us but ourselves, no one can and no one may.' In Buddhism, salvation is something that is not external. To be happy, and at peace, Buddhism says, we have to be vigilant, aware of ourselves. *Mindful*. 'As rain breaks through an ill-thatched house, passion in the sense of suffering will break through an unreflecting mind.'

In a world with far more shiny distractions than the world of Himalayan India way over two thousand years ago, our metaphorical mental houses may be harder to thatch than ever before.

Our minds now are less like thatched houses and a bit like computers. Yes, I could in theory get on my computer, open a Word document and just write, but I would probably check Facebook, Twitter, Instagram, the Guardian website. I might — if I am going through a neurotic patch — do a quick ego search, or check out any new Goodreads or Amazon reviews of my books or go on Google and type in a list of real or imaginary ailments to see which terminal disease I am currently suffering from.

Even Buddha himself would struggle these days, though the lack of Wi-Fi in the Himalayan foothills would be a blessing if you wanted to meditate for forty-nine days under a tree.

One thing I do understand, though, is that more is not *better*. I am not a Buddhist. I find all strict and certain guidelines too scary. Life is beautiful in its ambiguity. But I like the idea of being alert to ourselves, of connecting to the universal rather than living life on a see-saw of hope and fear.

For me personally, happiness isn't about abandoning the world of *stuff*, but in appreciating it for what it is. We cannot save ourselves from suffering by buying an iPhone. That doesn't mean we shouldn't buy one, it just means we should know such things are not ends in themselves.

And compassion.

That's another thing I like about Buddhism.

The idea that kindness makes us happier than selfishness. That kindness is a shredding of the self or, in Schopenhauer-speak, will — that releases us from the suffering that is our desires and wants.

To be self*less*, while being mind*ful*, seems to be a good solution, when the self intensifies and causes us to suffer.

Being good feels good because it makes us remember that we are not the only person that matters in this world. We all matter because we are all alive. And so kindness is an active way in which we can see and feel the bigger picture. We are ultimately all the same thing. We are life. We are consciousness. And so by feeling part of humanity, rather than an isolated unit, we feel better. We might physically perish, like a cell in a body might perish, but the body of life continues. And so, in the sense that life is a shared experience, we continue.

Self-help

How to stop time: kiss.
How to travel in time: read.
How to escape time: music.
How to feel time: write.
How to release time: breathe.

Thoughts on time

Time troubles us.

It is because of time that we grow old, and because of time we die. These are worrying things. As Aristotle put it, 'time crumbles things'. And we are scared of our own crumbling, and the crumbling of others.

We feel an urgency to get on because time is short. To 'just do it', as Nike said. But is *doing* the answer? Or does doing actually speed up time? Wouldn't it be better just to *be*, even if less sporty footwear ends up being sold?

Time does go at different speeds. As I've said, the few months in 1999 and 2000 when I was deeply ill felt like years. Decades, even. Pain lengthens time. But that is only because pain forces us to be aware of it.

Being aware of other things also helps lengthen time. This is all meditation is. Awareness of ourselves in the 'amber' of the moment, to use Kurt Vonnegut's term. It sounds easy, but how much of our lives are we actually living in the present? How much instead are we either excited or worrying about the future, or regretting or mourning the past? Our response to all this worry about time is to try and achieve things before it is too late. Gain money, improve our status, marry, have children, get a promotion, gain more money, on and on for ever. Or rather, not for ever. If it were for ever, we wouldn't be having this discussion. But we kind of know that turning life into a desperate race for more stuff is only going to shorten it. Not in years, not in terms of actual time, but in terms of how time feels. Imagine all the time we had was bottled up, like wine, and handed over to us. How would we make that bottle last? By sipping slowly, appreciating the taste, or by gulping?

Formentera

To the south of Ibiza there is the small island of Formentera, fourth-largest of the Balearic Islands. Me and Andrea used to go there sometimes on rare days off. It was a place of white beaches and pristine water — the cleanest in the whole Mediterranean due to UNESCO-protected seagrasses under the water. It was the calming yin to Ibiza's frenetic yang. Its small population of two thousand people is dotted liberally with artists, hippies and yoga instructors (if you look at it on the map you'll see it is shaped like an upside down V, as if the island is continually in downward dog pose). It retained a sixties vibe. Bob Dylan spent some time living in the lighthouse at Cap de Barbaria, on the island's southernmost tip. Formentera was also where Joni Mitchell wrote the album *Blue*.

I used to have a phobia about the Balearics. Couldn't face the idea of them, as it was on Ibiza that I began to fall apart. But now when I think of a calm place, I think of here. I picture its landscape of juniper and almond trees. I think of that sea as well. So bright and blue and clear.

I think of the names of its small villages, and harbour, and beaches. Es Pujol, El Pilar de la Mola, La Savina, Cap de Barbaria, Playa Illetes. And, most evocative of all, the name of the island itself.

When I feel the tension rising I sometimes close my eyes and think of it, the word rolling like soft pristine saltwater against sand. *Formentera, Formentera, Formentera* . . .

Images on a screen

In the old days, before the breakdown, I used to deal with worry by distracting myself. By going out to clubs, by drinking heavily, by spending summers in Ibiza, by wanting the spiciest food, the brashest movies, the edgiest novels, the loudest music, the latest nights. I was scared of the quiet. I was scared, I suppose, of having to slow down and soften the volume. Scared of having nothing but my own mind to listen to.

But after I became ill, all of this was suddenly out of bounds. I once switched on the radio and heard pounding house music and it gave me a panic attack. If I ate a jalfrezi, I would lie in bed that night hallucinating and palpitating. People talk about using alcohol and drugs to self-medicate, and I would have loved to dull my senses. I would have taken crack if I thought it would help me ignore the hurricane in my head. But from the age of twenty-four to thirty-two I didn't have so much as a single glass of wine. Not because I was strong (as my teetotal future mother-in-law always thought I was) but because I was petrified of anything that would alter my mind. I went five of those years refusing even to take an ibuprofen. Not because I had been drunk off my head when I first became ill — the day I became ill I hadn't had so much as a sip of alcohol and was in a (comparatively) healthy patch. I suppose it was just that feeling that my damaged mind lay precariously in the balance, like the bus hanging off the edge of a cliff in *The Italian Job*, and that the gold/alcohol might look tempting but to reach for it would be to send yourself falling towards a fatal end.

So, this was the problem. Just when I really needed to take my mind off something, I couldn't. My fear was such that even after smelling a glass of Andrea's red wine I would imagine those inhaled molecules entering my brain and tilting it further away from me.

But this was a good thing. It meant I had to focus on my mind. Like in an old horror movie, I was pulling back the curtain and seeing the monster.

Years later, I would read books on mindfulness and meditation, and realise that the key to happiness — or that even more desired thing, *calmness* — lies not in always thinking happy thoughts. No. That is impossible. No mind on earth with any kind of intelligence could spend a lifetime enjoying only happy thoughts. The key is in accepting your thoughts, all of them, even the bad ones. Accept thoughts, but don't become them.

Understand, for instance, that having a sad thought, even having a continual succession of sad thoughts, is not the same as being a sad person. You can walk through a storm and feel the wind but you know you are not the wind.

That is how we must be with our minds. We must allow ourselves to feel their gales and downpours, but all the time knowing this is just necessary weather.

When I sink deep, now, and I still do from time to time, I try and understand that there is another, bigger and stronger part of me that is not sinking. It stands unwavering. It is, I suppose, the part that would have been once called my soul.

We don't have to call it that, if we think it has too many connotations. We can call it simply a self. Let's just understand this. If we are tired or hungry or hungover, we are likely to be in a bad mood. That bad mood is therefore not really us. To believe in the things we feel at that point is wrong, because those feelings would disappear with food or sleep.

But when I was at my lowest points I

touched something solid, something hard and strong at the core of me. Something imperishable, immune to the changeability of thought. The self that is not only I but also we. The self that connects me to you, and human to human. The hard, unbreakable force of survival. Of life. Of the 150,000 generations of us that have gone before, and of those yet to be born. Our human essence. Just as the ground below New York and, say, Lagos, becomes identical if you go down far enough beneath the earth's surface, so every human inhabitant on this freak wonder of a planet shares the same core.

I am you and you are me. We are alone, but not alone. We are trapped by time, but also infinite. Made of flesh, but also stars.

Smallness

I went back to visit my parents in Newark about a month ago. They don't live in the same house, but the street they are on is parallel to the street where we used to live. It is a five-minute walk.

The corner shop is still there. I walked there *on my own* and bought a newspaper and could happily wait for the shopkeeper to give me my change. The houses I passed were the same orange brick houses. Nothing much had changed. Nothing makes you feel smaller, more trivial, than such a vast transformation inside your own mind while the world carries on, oblivious. Yet nothing is more freeing. To accept your smallness in the world.

How to live (forty pieces of advice I feel to be helpful but which I don't always follow)

1. Appreciate happiness when it is there.

2. Sip, don't gulp.

3. Be gentle with yourself. Work less. Sleep more.

4. There is absolutely nothing in the past that you can change. That's basic physics.

5. Beware of Tuesdays. And Octobers.

6. Kurt Vonnegut was right. 'Reading and writing are the most nourishing forms of meditation anyone has so far found.'

7. Listen more than you talk.

8. Don't feel guilty about being idle. More harm is probably done to the world through work than idleness.But perfect your idleness. Make it mindful.

9. Be aware that you are breathing.

10. Wherever you are, at any moment, try and find something beautiful. A face, a line out of a poem, the clouds out of a window, some graffiti, a wind farm. Beauty cleans the mind.

11. Hate is a pointless emotion to have inside you. It is like eating a scorpion to punish it for stinging you.

12. Go for a run. Then do some yoga.

13. Shower before noon.

14. Look at the sky. Remind yourself of the cosmos. Seek vastness at every opportunity, in order to see the smallness of yourself.

15. Be kind.

16. Understand that thoughts are thoughts. If they are unreasonable, reason with them, even if you have no reason left. You are the observer of your mind, not its victim.

17. Do not watch TV aimlessly. Do not go on social media aimlessly. Always be aware of what you are doing, and why you are doing it. Don't value TV less. Value it more. Then you will watch it less. Unchecked distractions will lead you to distraction.

18. Sit down. Lie down. Be still. Do nothing. Observe. Listen to your mind. Let it do what it does without judging it. Let it go, like the Snow Queen in *Frozen*.

19. Don't worry about things that probably won't happen.

20. Look at trees. Be near trees. Plant trees. (Trees are great.)

21. Listen to that yoga instructor on YouTube, and 'walk as if you are kissing the Earth with your feet'.

22. Live. Love. Let go. The three Ls.

23. Alcohol maths. Wine multiplies itself by itself. The more you have, the more you are likely to have. And if it's hard to stop at one glass, it will be impossible at three. Addition is multiplication.

24. Beware of the gap. The gap between where you are and where you want to be. Simply thinking of the gap widens it. And you end up falling through.

25. Read a book without thinking about finishing it. Just read it. Enjoy every word, sentence, and paragraph. Don't wish for it to end, or for it to never end.

26. No drug in the universe will make you feel better, at the deepest level, than being kind to other people.

27. Listen to what Hamlet — literature's most famous depressive — told Rosencrantz and Guildenstern. 'There is nothing either good or bad, but thinking makes it so.'

28. If someone loves you, let them. Believe in that love. Live for them, even when you feel there is no point.

29. You don't need the world to understand you. It's fine. Some people will never really understand things they haven't experienced. Some will. Be grateful.

30. Jules Verne wrote of the 'Living Infinite'. This is the world of love and emotion that is like a 'sea'. If we can submerge ourselves in it, we find infinity in ourselves, and the space we need to survive.

31. Three in the morning is never the time to try and sort out your life.

32. Remember that there is nothing weird about you. You are just a human, and everything you do and feel is a natural thing, because we are natural animals. You are nature. You are a hominid ape. You are in

the world and the world is in you. Everything connects.

33. Don't believe in good or bad, or winning and losing, or victory and defeat, or up and down. At your lowest and at your highest, whether you are happy or despairing or calm or angry, there is a kernel of you that stays the same. That is the you that matters.

34. Don't worry about the time you lose to despair. The time you will have afterwards has just doubled its value.

35. Be transparent to yourself. Make a greenhouse for your mind. Observe.

36. Read Emily Dickinson. Read Graham Greene. Read Italo Calvino. Read Maya Angelou. Read anything you want. Just read. Books are possibilities. They are escape routes. They give you options when you have none. Each one can be a home for an uprooted mind.

37. If the sun is shining, and you can be outside, *be outside*.

38. Remember that the key thing about life on earth is change. Cars rust. Paper yellows. Technology dates. Caterpillars become butterflies. Nights morph into days. Depression lifts.

39. Just when you feel you have no time to relax, know that this is the moment you most need to make time to relax.

40. Be brave. Be strong. Breathe, and keep going. You will thank yourself later.

Things I have enjoyed since the time I thought I would never enjoy anything again

Sunrises, sunsets, the thousand suns and worlds that aren't ours but shine in the night sky. Books. Cold beer. Fresh air. Dogs. Horses. Yellowing paperbacks. Skin against skin at one in the morning. Long, deep, meaningful kisses. Short, shallow, polite kisses. (All kisses.) Cold swimming pools. Oceans. Seas. Rivers. Lakes. Fjords. Ponds. Puddles. Roaring fires. Pub meals. Sitting outside and eating olives. The lights fading in the cinema, with a bucket of warm popcorn in your lap. Music. Love. Unabashed emotion. Rock pools. Swimming pools. Peanut butter sandwiches. The scent of pine on a warm evening in Italy. Drinking water after a long run. Getting the all-clear after a health scare. Getting *the* phone call. Will Ferrell in *Elf*. Talking to the person who knows me best. Pigeon pose. Picnics. Boat rides. Watching my son being born. Catching my daughter in the water during her first three seconds. Reading *The Tiger Who Came to Tea*, and doing the tiger's voice. Talking politics with my parents. *Roman Holiday* (and a Roman holiday). Talking Heads. Talking online about depression for the first time, and getting a good response. Kanye West's first album (I know, I know). Country music (country music!). The Beach Boys. Watching old soul singers on YouTube. Lists. Sitting on a bench in the park on a sunny day. Meeting writers I love. Foreign roads. Rum cocktails. Jumping up and down (they're publishing my book, they're publishing my book, *Jesus Christ, they're publishing my book*). Watching every Hitchcock movie. Cities twinkling at night as you drive past them, as if they are fallen constellations of stars. Laughing. Yes. Laughing so hard it hurts. Laughing as you bend forward and as your abdomen actually starts to hurt from so much pleasure, so much release, and then as you sit back and audibly groan and inhale deeply, staring at the person next to you, mopping up the joy. Reading a new Geoff Dyer book. Reading an old Graham Greene book. Running down hills. Christmas trees. Painting the walls of a new house. White wine. Dancing at three in the morning. Vanilla fudge. Wasabi peas. My children's terrible jokes. Watching geese and goslings on the river. Reaching an age — thirty-five, thirty-six, thirty-seven, thirty-eight, thirty-nine — I never thought

I'd reach. Talking to friends. Talking to strang-
ers. Talking to you. Writing this book.

Thank you.

Further Reading

Bad Pharma: How medicine is broken, and how we can fix it, Ben Goldacre (Fourth Estate, 2012)

An eye-opening look at the pharmaceutical industry and the vested interests at play.

Darkness Visible: A Memoir of Madness, William Styron (Vintage, 2001)

This classic memoir from 1989, which references *Paradise Lost* in the title, is beautifully written and — given the author's experience on the sleeping pill Halcion — serves as a reminder of the dangers of taking the wrong medication.

The Depths: The Evolutionary Origins of the Depression Epidemic, Jonathan Rottenberg (Basic Books, 2014)

The best look at depression from an evolutionary perspective that I've come across.

Madness and Civilzation, Michel Foucault (Routledge Classics, 2006)

A controversial, eccentric work, more interested in society than the mind, but still a thought-provoking read.

The Man Who Couldn't Stop: OCD and the true story of a life lost in thought, Dr David Adam (Picador, 2014)

A brilliant and at times highly personal study of OCD, full of insights into the mind.

Making Friends with Anxiety: A warm, supportive little book to ease worry and panic, Sarah Rayner (CreateSpace, 2014)

Simple, lucid advice on how to accept your anxiety.

Mindfulness: A practical guide to finding peace in a frantic world, Professor Mark Williams and Dr Danny Penman (Piatkus, 2011)

Mindfulness has its fair share of sceptics, but as a way of adding punctuation into the breathless sentence of your life, I find it can be very useful. This is a solid guide.

The Noonday Demon: An anatomy of depression, Andrew Solomon (Chatto & Windus, 2001)

An astonishing (occasionally terrifying) account of Solomon's experience of depression. It is particularly good on diagnosis and treatment.

Sane New World: Taming the Mind, Ruby Wax (Hodder, 2014)

A clear and instructive book, with a strong emphasis on mindfulness as a way through and as funny as you'd expect from Ruby Wax.

Why Zebras Don't Get Ulcers: The Acclaimed Guide to Stress, Stress-Related Diseases, and Coping, Dr Robert M. Sapolsky (Henry Holt, 2004)

A very interesting take on stress, and how it builds up, and the physical body.

A note, and some acknowledgements

Willie Nelson once said that sometimes you have to either write a song or you kick your foot through a window. The third option, I suppose, is that you write a book.

And I have felt the need to write *this* book for a long time. But I have also been worried about writing it because it is obviously quite personal and I worried that writing it would make me relive some of those bad times. So for a long time I have been writing about it indirectly, in fiction.

Two years ago I wrote a book called *The Humans*. It was in that novel, more than in any of my others, in which I addressed my own breakdown. The story was technically traditional science fiction — an alien arrives on Earth in human form and slowly changes his view of humanity — but I was really writing about the alienation of depression and how you get over that and how you can end up loving the world again.

In a note in the end of that book, the equivalent of right here, I publically 'came

241

out' and talked very briefly of my own experience of panic disorder and depression. Just that little bit of openness met with a warm response, and I realised I'd been worrying over nothing. Rather than make me feel like a weirdo, being open had made me realise how many people suffer similar experiences at some time or other. Just as none of us are 100% physically healthy no one is 100% mentally healthy. We are all on a scale.

I then had the confidence to write a bit more about my experience online. But I still didn't know if I would ever write this book. The person who told me to was the great Cathy Rentzenbrink. Cathy is one of the most dynamic and, frankly, brilliant advocates of books, championing their cause and — in this case — causing them to exist. She was the person, who, over some Wasabi-flavoured popcorn at a branch of Itsu, told me to write a book about depression. So, here it is, Cathy. Hope you like it.

This book would not have been *this* book without an editor. (The main advantage of books over life is that they can be redrafted and redrafted, whereas life, alas, is always a first draft.) It is the obligatory thing to acknowledge your editor in the acknowledgements but even if it wasn't, ethics and logic would demand I mention Francis Bickmore's role in shaping this book. There are numerous suggestions he made that helped me work out how to write it. Mainly though, I was grateful to have an editor who would be fine with the genre-straddling nature of this book, who wouldn't ask, 'is it a memoir or a self-help book or an overview?' And who would be fine about it being a bit of all those things.

And for me, this makes Canongate the perfect publishers. I feel like I can do something different and, if they like it, they'll go with it. So I'm blessed to be with them. They turned my career around, and I am thankful to the legendary Jamie Byng and everyone who works there (Jenny Todd, Andrea Joyce, Katie Moffat, Jaz Lacey-Campbell, Anna Frame, Vicki Rutherford, Sian Gibson, Jo Dingley and the whole gang) for taking that chance on me and getting behind my stuff the way they have.

Okay, this spirit of stifling gushiness must continue, while I thank Clare Conville, my agent, who totally *got* the book and reassured me when I was still very nervous about it. She is a formidable person to have on your side, and was vital in helping steer *Reasons to Stay Alive* on the right course.

Also thanks to everyone who has helped

and supported me and my writing in various ways over the years. Tanya Seghatchian, Jeanette Winterson, Stephen Fry, SJ Watson, Joanne Harris, Julia Kingsford, Natalie Doherty, Annie Eaton, Amanda Craig, Caradoc King, Amanda Ross, and many, many more. Also thanks to all those booksellers that I have met and who have gone the extra mile. An obvious mention here for Leilah Skelton, from Waterstones Doncaster, who made jars of peanut butter and special badges in honour of *The Humans*. Also to everyone on Facebook and Twitter who has helped spread the word, especially those tweeters who contributed to the #reasonstostayalive chapter.

I've always had an open and loving family and I thank them for helping me stay afloat, but also for being totally okay about me writing this book. So infinite thanks and love as always to Mum, Dad and Phoebe, as well as Freda, Albert, David and Katherine too. Thank you for being my net. I love all of you.

Thanks to Lucas and Pearl, for giving me a thousand reasons every day.

And of course, Andrea. For everything.

Permissions credits

We do hope that you have enjoyed reading
this large print book.

Did you know that all of our titles
are available for purchase?

We publish a wide range of high quality
large print books including:
Romances, Mysteries, Classics
General Fiction
Non Fiction and Westerns

Special interest titles available in
large print are:
The Little Oxford Dictionary
Music Book
Song Book
Hymn Book
Service Book

Also available from us courtesy of
Oxford University Press:
Young Readers' Dictionary
(large print edition)
Young Readers' Thesaurus
(large print edition)

For further information or a free
brochure, please contact us at:
Ulverscroft Large Print Books Ltd.,
The Green, Bradgate Road, Anstey,
Leicester, LE7 7FU, England.
Tel: (00 44) 0116 236 4325
Fax: (00 44) 0116 234 0205

AN ACT OF LOVE

Marie Fleming and Sue Leonard

Described by the High Court President as one of the most remarkable witnesses to ever come before the courts, Marie Fleming, diagnosed with multiple sclerosis in her mid-thirties, became a household name with her trailblazing campaign and legal challenge for the right to die with dignity. Here, she tells the personal story behind the public face — from her young years growing up in Donegal, as she struggled to keep her family together after her mother left, to her battle as a teenager to hold on to her baby daughter, and her later quest for education and self-betterment against the odds.

PICKED UP, PATCHED UP AND SENT HOME

Carl Walker

Like so many people, Carl Walker has used the NHS for a number of reasons throughout his life — some serious, others less so. From being caught red-handed testing a stethoscope on himself, and (unsuccessfully) attempting to remove a friend's ingrown toenail with a pair of pliers, to the health visitor who offers guidance that soothes Carl's newborn and restores sanity to his household, the specialists who help him manage his epilepsy, and the GP who assures him the worrying lump is not cancer, here are stories that speak to the experiences of normal folk, and remind us just what an amazing thing a public national health service really is.

RUNNING LIKE A GIRL

Alexandra Heminsley

Defeated by gyms and bored with yoga, Alexandra Heminsley decided to run — with high hopes of attaining the arse of an athlete, the waist of a supermodel, and the speed of a gazelle. Her first attempt did not end well. Yet, six years later, she had run five marathons in two continents. This is not just a book about running. It's about ambition (getting out of bed on a rainy Sunday morning counts), relationships (including talking to the intimidating staff in the trainer shop), and your body (your boobs *don't* have to wobble when you run). And it's also about realising that you can do more than you ever thought possible . . .